FIRED TO INSPIRED

FIRED to *Inspired*

A WOMAN'S TRANSFORMATION
ONE BRAVE STEP AT A TIME

KIMBERLY CLINE

Fired to Inspired
Copyright ©2015

All rights reserved. No part of this book may be reproduced, stored or transmitted in any form or by any means, electronic or mechanical including photocopying, recording or by any information storage and retrieval system, without permission in writing from the author, except by a reviewer who may quote brief passages for review purposes. Inquiries should be sent to the author at www.KimberlyCline.com

First Printing 2015
Prosperity Place LLC

Fired to Inspired PAPERBACK ISBN: 978-0-9964473-0-0
Fired to Inspired HARD COVER ISBN: 978-0-9964473-1-7
Fired to Inspired E-BOOK ISBN: 978-0-9964473-2-4

COVER DESIGN BY CHRISTINE TALLEY
www.gruvcreative.com

ILLUSTRATIONS BY TRACEY LYON
www.TraceyLyon.com

BOOK DESIGN BY KIMBERLY CLINE
www.KimberlyCline.com

ACKNOWLEDGEMENTS

I am filled with so much gratitude, I want to use this page to thank the wonderful people who helped me with this project. This has been an incredible journey, filled with the most amazing and supportive souls to bring *Fired to Inspired* to life.

First, I must thank my bestie Linda Sacha for not only being the most wonderful friend a gal could ever have, but for her generosity in sharing her knowledge and experience in the *Writer's Success Series* that inspired me and so many others to complete the projects and passions in our hearts. Sacha lovingly guided me through the entire process as I aligned my body, mind, and spirit.

Christine Talley was able to capture the images in my head to create a book cover that would inspire me through the writing process.

My mom Carol was ready and willing to jump in with both feet and serve as the first-line grammarian.

Vickie Pleus and Audra Jolliffe are each a ball of fire and continue to keep one under me. Audra was a safe person to start the editing process with, and Vickie's public relations and communication skills were invaluable for transforming a bunch of pages into chapters.

Certified Zentangle® teacher, friend and soul sister Tracey Lyon blessed me and all of us with beautiful graphics to add some eye candy to each chapter.

I am grateful to Kathleen Rasche for her support and mentoring through the editing and publishing process. She held my hand and cheered me on every step of the way.

Kim Meadows gifted me with her editing services to move this project along.

Keith Allen wrapped up the editing process with his amazing proofreading skills so I can rest a little easier now, sending this project to press.

Cassandra Poertner talked me down from the ledge and made sure all my print files were converted and formatted properly.

Last, but certainly not least, is husband Michael. He may never read this book, but his love and support are always there and makes feel unstoppable.

HOW TO USE THIS BOOK

Let me tell you, I am ***inspired*** and **on fire** to share this book with you! Writing this page is proof to me we're in the homestretch and almost ready to go to press.

As you will discover while reading *Fired to Inspired*, I haven't done anything earth-shattering (although many will be shocked at how many times I've been married). I've not battled a terminal illness or achieved huge financial success. I have simply gone through this roller-coaster ride we call life, experiencing what I imagine many people do, too. In short, *I get knocked down, but I get up again* (thank you for the lyrical guidance, Chumbawamba).

While writing this book, more and more was revealed to me about my life, and the path I have traveled. I was awe-struck to see the connectivity in my life and purpose that has been inside me all along. I believe that in each of our lives, many answers have already been revealed to us; we just need to remember them, and honor the lessons with gratitude.

At the end of each chapter, you'll find "Fan the Flame" prompts; they include questions that reflect some of my discoveries in the chapter. Each question invites you to discover or remember the embers in your heart. Sometimes it takes a little work to excavate them, but answers will be revealed. Trust what your inner voice wants to share with you, and growth and understanding will be yours.

FOREWORD

When my husband retired, we decided to leave New England and move to Central Florida. After loads of consideration, we knew we wanted to live in a midsize town that had a college (or one nearby), and a downtown area that felt quirky and cozy with a sense of community. We hit the road with a list of five towns to visit as we sought the perfect match. Four towns down, we were feeling discouraged, as none had met the criteria. Then we pulled into DeLand, Florida.

 We were sipping a lovely beverage at an outdoor table and noticed the sidewalks rapidly filling up with hundreds of cheery residents. Little did we know that we were about to witness the amazing annual spectacle of the DeLand Dog Parade. That was it; we were sold. Happy people, happy pets, crazy costumes and floats, great places to sip and a palpable feeling of pride and fun … all nestled on a lovely "Main Street," along with beautiful Stetson University. We moved to DeLand two months later.

 When you leave one life behind and transport yourself to a new community across the country, your greatest hope is that the town is home to people you want to call your friends. As an author and a life coach, my professional life is spent on the phone or in front of the computer — not exactly a great way to develop one's new social life. Certain I would have to do something radical like become a Brownie leader, join a church, or coach a croquet team just to meet some humans, I was suddenly spared. I met Kimberly Cline.

 To say Kim is outgoing, fun, forward-thinking, generous and connecting is an understatement. It's an understatement like, "The Pope is religious." Of course, for all these reasons, I instantly adored her, but it was something more that I experienced — and continue to experience with her — that soon made us "besties." It was her courage. I was and still am in awe of her absolute bravery to face an obstacle that most of us would scream and run from, and turn it into an invitation for transformation, profit and fun that supports others.

Kim's journey from being fired to being an award-winning entrepreneur on that Main Street in DeLand is one that reminds us all that if we want something bad enough, we can make it so. That doesn't happen overnight; it all unfolds as we boldly move through each of our small and giant fears.

Each day, we have an opportunity to despise or treasure the less–than–great aspects of our yesterdays that created our fears in the first place. That daily choice is what moves us forward or not. When we choose to own the fact that the strength of our personal fiber is based on the thousands of threads that have woven us into the beings that we are in this moment, the possibilities are endless. The more we can love and appreciate the fullness of who we are, the more we can cherish today.

There's nothing like hearing how a fellow human has taken this journey. I am certain that Kim's authenticity and vulnerability in sharing all her threads will inspire you as it has me and hundreds of others. And please do come to DeLand; the parade and our eclectic Main Street won't let you down. Come meet my bestie, Kimberly Cline.

Linda Sacha
www.LindaSacha.com

TABLE OF CONTENTS

WHY *FIRED TO INSPIRED*? 1

BURNING EMBERS THE HEART REMEMBERS 5

MY INNER VOICE:
SHOULD I TRUST THAT CRAZY CHICK? 9

SPARKING UP FRIENDSHIPS:
THE TRANSFORMATION TRIBE 13

THOSE INNER ARTIST'S HOT SPOTS 21

IT'S GETTING HOT IN HERE.. 27

THE SLOW BURN (I CALL IT 'HIGH SCHOOL') 31

WOO HOO! I'M EMPLOYABLE!
(THAT'S A GOOD THING, I THINK.) 37

WHERE THERE'S SMOKE, THERE'S 'FIRED' 41

OUT OF HELL, AND INTO A HOT 'TRUNK' 47

RAPID-FIRE CHANGE:
THE FUNKY TRUNK COMBUSTION 51

THERE SHE IS AGAIN:
THE INNER VOICE SPEAKETH 55

THE CONTROLLED BURN:
SETTING PARAMETERS FOR MY BUSINESS 61

LEADERS CAN STAND THE HEAT,
SO WHY AM I SO CHILLY? 63

GIVING MYSELF PERMISSION: IT'S TIME TO MOVE 67

I AM PROSPEROUS – DARN IT! 73

LET THAT FLAME GROW TALLER, LADIES! 77

MEET THE MANIFESTING MAVEN (THAT'S ME!) 81

FROM COMBUSTION TO REFLECTION:
MORE CHANGES COME FOR FUNKY TRUNK 87

THE PURPOSE OF THE FLAMES 91

CONFUSED NO MORE:
REMOVING THE SMOKE SCREENS 95

HONORING THE TEMPLE: IT'S TIME TO GET FIT 99

ON FIRE AND INSPIRED...FOREVER 105

WHAT'S NEXT FOR KIM POSSIBLE? 107

WHY *FIRED TO INSPIRED*?

My friend Sacha suggested I write a book and call it *Funky Trunk Wisdom*, after witnessing firsthand all the decisions, challenges and triumphs I've been through opening my own retail business, Funky Trunk Treasures. Sacha felt certain I was doing something really special to promote and mentor local artists. She also believes I've done something amazing by getting out of corporate life, getting over my insecurities and by empowering myself in a way I never thought possible. Quite honestly, I wasn't really seeing things the same way. I was just doing what I felt guided to do and what seemed to come naturally. To me, it really wasn't that big of a deal.

    The more I thought about writing, the more it intrigued me. My thought process was, *"Wow, wouldn't it be cool to write a book? I have something to say."* Then I asked myself, *"Would people really care what Kimberly Cline has to say? I mean, so many people have started businesses."* I could think of so many things to write about. If I could just narrow down the topic and go, I might end up with a book, and maybe people would buy it, and maybe, just

> "I was just doing what I felt guided to do and what seemed to come naturally."

maybe, some big publishing company would want to publish it, and I could end up on *Oprah* or *Ellen*. We've all had that fantasy, right?

Well, that was a year ago, and what a difference a year makes. After celebrating our second anniversary in business at Funky Trunk Treasures, I experienced a huge shift in my world. I started to pay myself and take time off to breathe. As far as writing a book, I came to realize that I am a woman with a message. I'm writing this book not only to share my experience with others, but to share it with *myself*. I am notorious for always looking to the next thing that I can do and how I can do it better. Rarely do I take a moment to look back and reflect on what I've accomplished.

I don't see myself as possessing any exceptional gifts. This journey has been all about learning to listen to my inner voice; there have been lots of conversations with God, and taking action despite my fears. To clarify, I use "God" and "Universe" interchangeably throughout the book. When I feel a direct connection or am being conversational, I use the word God. When referring to the energy or omnipresence, I usually use Universe. *Fired to Inspired* was written so I can acknowledge my journey, process and growth while hopefully inspiring others to do the same.

Many of us constantly question whether or not we are on the right path and struggle to discover our purpose. I now know that the clues are there if only we learn to listen and trust in ourselves. If we're lucky, the Universe may intervene on our behalf with one event that will shift everything. I am grateful for the healing and lessons I've experienced along the way and even more grateful for how gentle they've been.

Today, I really understand what an entrepreneur is, and I know how to spell it too! I hope *Fired to Inspired* will inspire you and help you discover the courage to follow your heart. It is my journey of how my life circumstances went from devastating to divine.

Fan the Flame

IS THERE A PIECE OF YOUR LIFE THAT YOU'D LIKE TO TRANSFORM?

WHAT DO YOU WISH WAS DIFFERENT?

WHAT WOULD IT TAKE TO FOLLOW YOUR HEART?

BURNING EMBERS THE HEART REMEMBERS

In 2007, about six months after I relocated to Central Florida, I began working for an accountant named Bob. Working for him was a true gift. He was honest and hardworking, and really wanted to help people. We got along famously. As a retired firefighter, he had a wicked sense of humor, and I admired how he was never shy about expressing his love for his family.

    I was single at the time. Bob gave me hope and modeled what I wanted in a relationship with somebody. I didn't really have any positive male role models growing up, so for me, Bob was like a father and a brother all rolled into one. He was a great listener and always supportive.

    As I was approaching three years working at his practice, the Universe gave me a nudge to move on, for seemingly no apparent reason. I went out on my own, providing marketing and image-consulting services for small businesses. I usually get an itch to make a change between two and three years at a job, but this felt different.

    Bob and I kept in touch. I became one of his clients and we met occasionally at one of his favorite spots for barbecue and a beer. We both served on the Foundation board for a local Adventist hospital. One time when we were out, Bob spotted the hospital director. Bob gently pushed his beer to my side of the table and smiled — never a dull moment with Bob. Sure, like the beer wasn't his.

> "So far away from home, I didn't feel the need to be brave for anyone."

Bob lost his life to cancer almost one year after I left his practice. Just six months prior to that day, his son, Daniel, also lost his battle with cancer. I was in England for holiday when I heard the news that Bob's cancer had returned. So far away from home, I didn't feel the need to be brave for anyone. I just broke down and sobbed to the point I could barely breathe. I refused to let my mind entertain thoughts of death. I wanted to stay positive for Bob. I wanted him to get a miracle, and the faster the better. As time passed, I still held on to the thought that maybe the doctors were wrong, maybe Bob could turn it around. I adored him. He made a huge impact on my life in a very short amount of time.

Now looking back, I can see the big picture clearer. I know that there was no way I could've been working for him and kept myself together during those sad times. I was able to visit Bob at home a few days before he passed away. We laughed and watched an episode of *Have Gun - Will Travel*, together in his living room. I am forever grateful to his wife for allowing me into her home to spend some time with this dear man.

Fan the Flame

WHAT ARE SOME MOMENTS IN YOUR LIFE WHEN YOU QUESTIONED GOD'S TIMING?

DID THE ANSWER YOU RECEIVED GIVE YOU PEACE?

ARE YOU STILL WAITING FOR AN ANSWER?

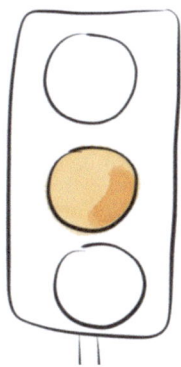

MY INNER VOICE: SHOULD I TRUST THAT CRAZY CHICK?

Still working on my own, in September 2011, I reluctantly accepted a part-time position with a company. Within a few months, I transitioned to full-time employment there as marketing coordinator. Interestingly, I wasn't looking for a job when I accepted the part-time position. I simply felt obligated to take it, since a friend had recommended me. It was one of those "why not" moments.

The position itself sounded, at first, like it was right up my alley. I definitely possessed the skills needed for the job, but when I went to the interview the one thing that really struck me was the weight of negative energy. It hit me as soon as I walked in the door. It radiated in the air. Instead of turning tail and running, I rationalized it and thought to myself, *"Maybe it's because of the décor or lack thereof."* But there was this little voice inside trying to get my attention. "Um, Kim, maybe this isn't such a good idea," it said. I ignored that voice and accepted the position.

When I started the job, I found out I had a great predecessor. It's like when you follow a brilliant older sibling through the school system and all your teachers think you should be just as smart. I challenged myself to get up to speed quickly and to see what I could do to take my job to the next level with skills I brought to the table. I just love to see things cleaned up, organized, and improved. At any job I've ever had, I have strived to keep things in such good order that anyone could come behind me, sit at my desk, and comfortably know what to do.

My boss was brilliant. I noticed that right off the bat. I also noticed I had an extremely difficult time working with her. I realized her job may have been all she had in her life, and that spurred my sense of compassion. In all my years of working various jobs, this was probably the most challenging I ever had. I kept telling myself that it afforded me a great opportunity to learn and grow. That nagging voice dissipated, but only for a short time.

As time passed, I felt like the very life was being sucked right out of me at this job. I was dying on the vine. There were a lot of unnecessary rules. At former jobs, I would have left before things got to this point. Despite my inner voice, I really felt there was something I was meant to learn from this experience. And maybe there was.

Looking back now, I can see how I had given up my internal power and was giving it to someone else. I wanted to break the cycle once and for all. Over time, I felt beaten and discounted as an intelligent human being. I tortured myself, feeling like I could never do anything right. Each day, I would come in fresh with new resolve, and think to myself, *"This is the day I'm turning things around."*

My husband Michael and I were newlyweds at the time and experiencing immigration issues from hell. He's British and had years ago abandoned the process to become a permanent resident. When we got married, he mistakenly used the wrong paperwork to re-initiate the process. After a trip to England, he was almost denied entry back into the States.

Because Michael wasn't yet able to legally work in this country, I needed my job. It didn't matter how I felt at work each day. I felt an even stronger sense of responsibility to keep it all together. So I sucked it up, put on the "big-girl panties," and continued to ignore my feelings. I felt disrespected, manipulated, and unappreciated. It was no one's fault really, just a bad fit. I'll never ignore my inner voice again.

Fan the Flame

DO YOU REMEMBER A TIME WHEN YOU IGNORED YOUR INNER VOICE?

WHAT WAS THE SITUATION?

WHAT HAPPENED WHEN YOU IGNORED THE VOICE?

WHAT DID YOU LEARN FROM THAT EXPERIENCE?

SPARKING UP FRIENDSHIPS: THE TRANSFORMATION TRIBE

In January 2012, my friend Cheryl gathered 10 women together and facilitated a 12-week program based on the book *The Artist's Way: A Spiritual Path to Higher Creativity* by Julia Cameron. I had been in an Artist's Way group more than 25 years ago and loved the book, the process, and the activities. I had tried several times to work through the book again on my own, but I never made it past the first chapter.

There is something about the group dynamic that allows each of us to open ourselves up, to share, and to support each other on the journey. When this new group met, I felt excited. I knew that every time I traveled this journey, additional insights would be revealed. And if I committed to the work, personal growth would happen.

I love growth; it's the getting to the growing part I hate. I hoped that by committing to a group this time I would pull my butt forward and it would offer me the clarity I needed to deal with my frustrations at work.

As the class progressed, I realized that I knew most of these women, but there was so much I didn't know *about* them. I loved and respected some, networked with a few, and previously worked with one. It was an amazing journey. I fell in love with each of them even more as they allowed themselves to be vulnerable. It was an awesome process to see each woman opening up and acknowledging herself and her gifts. We named ourselves the *Transformation Tribe*.

At the beginning of the 12-week growing process, I noticed that these women had each made some type of reference to their "closet." Those closets are where they hid their artwork from college, stored their art supplies, and kept their identity. They hadn't peeked inside for years except as a sacred place to escape, to be alone, and to have a margarita or two!

Only a few of my new close friends acknowledged themselves as artists. I found this very interesting. In all the years that I loved being behind the camera, I had never acknowledged myself as a photographer. That seemed a little strange to anyone who knew me. I have been doing photography for years and most of the time was compensated for my work. But, for some reason, if someone asked what I did, I struggled to say, "I'm a photographer." I felt like a liar. My mind would go crazy: "*When people find out the truth, they're going to laugh at me or, worse, they'll turn their backs on me. Who was I to call myself a photographer? There are a lot of photographers out there who are much more talented than me.*"

Sometime during the group meetings, I was asked by a massage therapist I knew if I would like to do a photography exhibit at her location during an upcoming art event. The town was planning an "Art Walk" in which artists displayed their work at various locations in our downtown district. Me, an artist? I usually speak before I think, so I immediately said yes. Did it really matter that she hadn't seen my photography and I didn't have a body of work to present? She had heard I was a photographer. Me, a photographer. I didn't think about the fact that I had never exhibited before. I was geeked to be acknowledged, not by the massage therapist, bless her soul, but by me. I am a photographer. No pressure, right? Since it was her first time hosting, and my first time exhibiting, I figured there wouldn't be any outrageous expectations.

Now, I had to get to work and create a plan. I asked myself, *"What would really get me excited?"* Years ago in a conversation I was having with God, I asked for guidance. I was guided to women's portraiture. Have you ever tried to rationalize something with God? I thought, *"Oh, no, that can't be. I mean, I would love photographing women, and it would bring so many creative possibilities. It's just that women are the most self-critical creatures. They would never be happy with the results."* Maybe God just couldn't see how difficult it would be to be paid and develop a prosperous business if I couldn't make the client happy. *"Well, God, thanks anyway. I think I will stick with weddings, family, and kid pictures. They are so much easier to market and produce."*

This time, I didn't ignore the call. I listened to my inner voice. I knew these amazing women, and more so since we became the Transformation Tribe. Maybe they would allow me to photograph them. I decided to center the photos around this "closet" theme. Everyone agreed to be a part of the exhibit, and I met with each woman individually to discuss the concept; I brainstormed with them to make them part of the process. I'll admit, I was nervous and scared during most of the project. I loved and admired these women so much. I didn't want to disappoint them … or myself.

> "Even today, friends ask me where I get the energy to move forward in the face of fear. I guess I really never knew I had a choice."

I planned as well as I could, and worked with my new photographer/artist mentor, Edson. A few months earlier, I had decided to take a Photoshop class at the local college, and Edson was the instructor. With his help, at the very least, I knew that I could feel confident on a technical level that this body of work would present well. I really stretched myself for this project. I realized when I am able to feel the fear and still just go for it in spite of being overwhelmed, when I am finished my sense of accomplishment gives me an incredible high.

The exhibit was called *"Transformations: Bringing Your Creativity Out of the Closet."* Everything I could have hoped for happened. Well over 100 people came to see the exhibit that night, the local newspaper showed up and printed a fabulous article with a ginormous photo of the Tribe holding their portraits, and a local television station came and did a short segment called "Making a Difference." It was exhilarating. While it was one of the scariest things I had ever done up to that point in my adult life, I felt like I was on to something here.

Until this experience, I never understood why creative people and artists didn't just create, sell, and promote their amazing work all the time so everyone could enjoy it. Sure, I knew there is nothing more intimidating than putting yourself and your creations out there for people to see. It's an extremely vulnerable feeling. When we allow ourselves to be vulnerable, we are opening ourselves up to judgment, criticism, and rejection.

On the flip side, when we are exposed in this way, we can open ourselves up to being loved, appreciated, and embraced for what we create and bring into this world. Being fearful can stop you right in your tracks. It can hold you back from all the possibilities. What a shame to miss out on all the fun. Even today, friends ask me where I get the energy to move forward in the face of fear. I guess I really never knew I had a choice. It's a journey. I'm moving forward. What's the big deal?

My work and I, synonymously speaking, were very well-received by the public; it was the Tribe's reaction that concerned me the most. Would they love the exhibit? Would they still love me? Their love and acceptance meant the most to me. I was on edge.

Overall, they were extremely supportive. Let's face it though, I was attempting to capture the transformation of these 10 women. The road sometimes got bumpy. Collectively, we were going through every type of transition you can imagine. We were going through separation from a spouse, death of a loved one, addictions, career changes, and scars from past abuse. We found our strength in each other, found the ability to nurture, and began to heal.

Even though we no longer meet each week, we stay connected and are supported by each other through every transition life brings. In this process I have learned that true friends support you no matter what, warts and all. Dealing with relationships and personalities, my feelings did get hurt; I could have closed myself off. I had certainly done that before. Instead I owned what was mine, and for once, did not own what was not mine. I broke that past pattern. So many times, I had cut myself off from relationships because I didn't know how to honor my feelings or stand up for myself. These ladies helped me find my inner courage to own my inner power. We were and still are the *Transformation Tribe!* I'm proud of us.

One night over pizza and wine with the Tribe, we fantasized for a moment about having a cool place downtown where people could come to take creative classes and workshops, buy from local artists, and just hang out. People would feel loved there, accepted for who they are. Besides a few restaurants, I had no idea what was even in our downtown district, or what the possibilities could be. One of the women mentioned a space downstairs from the Women's Museum that was vacant. Heck, I didn't even know we had a Women's Museum! I asked Sacha, who is also in the Tribe, "Hey, what do you think about having a retail space downtown?" She replied, "No, thank you, been there, done that." So I thought, *OK, never mind*. It must not be as good of an idea as I had thought.

Each week in the Artist's Way class, we were given tasks that helped us to go back in time and get in touch with our younger selves. Needless to say, these activities brought up a lot of deep issues. But they also helped with our healing process as it pertained to our creativity. Looking back, I am amazed at all I had forgotten.

Fan the Flame

HOW HAVE FEMALE FRIENDSHIPS MADE YOUR LIFE RICHER OR MORE FULFILLING?

WHAT DO YOU MOST CHERISH IN YOUR RELATIONSHIPS WITH OTHER WOMEN?

HOW DOES VULNERABILITY FIT INTO YOUR FRIENDSHIPS?

WHAT ABOUT THE QUALITY AND QUANTITY OF YOUR FEMALE RELATIONSHIPS?

THOSE INNER ARTIST'S HOT SPOTS

Yes, some of my childhood memories aren't great; many people's aren't. But the ones that I think of as being the best are the ones where a teacher recognized talent in me that I may never have noticed in myself. In the third grade, for example, I had just finished a geometric drawing of triangles. I used green, yellow and orange in the work.

My teacher, Mrs. Tilton, looked down and said, "You're very creative." Me? Really? How powerful words can be! Her statement about my creativity has stayed with me all my life and, interestingly enough, green, yellow, and orange are still my favorite colors. My friends tease me because they can pick out my artwork a mile away. Before the Tribe, I had never felt comfortable calling myself an artist, but I had no problem saying I was creative. Mrs. Tilton said I was.

That small experience set the stage for me. In middle school, I loved any art class I could take. My poetry was published in our yearbook, and I loved drawing. I hear people every day say they cannot draw, and I would chime in and agree, "I know; me too." Then I thought back to one of my favorite art classes. I remember a teacher who would draw a different

Disney character in each class, and we, his eager students, would follow along. As long as you paid attention and followed directions, you could do a decent job mimicking his drawing, and I did. I was proud that my rendition looked so close to the teacher's. I get that same thrill today when I learn from other artists in classes at what I fondly call "Funky U," the university of classes and workshops I offer at my shop.

Unfortunately, while being a creative kid, I was sidelined by other responsibilities. My mom was a single parent, which prompted me to take on adult responsibilities at a young age, so housekeeping and cooking were already part of my world by the time I hit middle school. Home Economics class was OK, but I found sewing to be a bit challenging. Thank goodness Mark Wisell, who used to sit in front of me in the fifth grade, showed mercy on me. He finished sewing the stuffed-frog class project I was so frustrated with. Today I think of him every time I see a frog. It makes me laugh. I had the best time in shop doing woodworking or using plastics. It was so much fun that I longed for my own jigsaw. I eventually got one.

During my high-school years, things got a little crazier. My mom remarried, and we moved a lot because of my stepfather's job. He worked for a car-rental agency. People would often ask me, "Are you an Army brat?" No, I was a rent-a-car brat … such brats are more accustomed to loaner cars than military bases.

I ended up going to five different high schools. Talk about pressure. First stop was Elk Grove Village High School in Illinois. I felt like a fish out of water, and I began to socially withdraw as a coping mechanism. My saving grace was rediscovering how much I enjoy photography. My grandfather had bought me a little toy camera when I was about 7 years old.

I was in awe of my older cousin David who I carefully watched at every family gathering when he would take family photos.

Being a freshman and new to the school, it took me a while to make some friends, but I did. There were Pam, Julie, Dee, Renate, and Chris; they were my best buddies. Thank goodness for them. We were so silly and nerdy. I still crack up thinking about that oh-so-awkward time. I also met my neighbor Debbie. Debbie was a senior. She lived with her mom and her brother, who was a year younger than me. I think I connected with her because she, like me, was the oldest sibling. I also had a younger brother and was living with a single mom. My mom had remarried just a few months before we moved to Illinois.

My parents divorced when I was very young, and my mom remarried when I was 13. I painfully remember the stigma placed on a divorced woman and a single mom in the early seventies.

Debbie was sweet and totally cool. We could talk about anything, and we talked about everything. My grandfather died about four months after we moved to Elk Grove Village. That meant we would be traveling back to Florida for the funeral. I was so anxious to talk to Debbie when I got back, but it was pretty late when we got home and school was in session the next day.

The next morning, I met my friends in the lunchroom before the bell rang, as always. They didn't seem particularly happy to see me and were acting kind of distant. I didn't pay too much attention; I kept telling them about my trip.

At one point, Chris asked me to go with her to the restroom. She proceeded to tell me that Debbie had been killed in a car accident over the

"I had never felt comfortable calling myself an artist, but I had no problem saying I was creative."

weekend. I was inconsolable. I broke down sobbing. I tried to calm down, but couldn't. I went to the office to call my mom and when she said she couldn't come get me, I was devastated. I had to stay at school and face my grief publicly that entire day. I was numb, with my face red and swollen from crying.

Feeling out of sorts without Debbie to talk with, I missed my old friends and my family and the life I once knew, the one I was supposed to have in Florida. I hated this new life. I was miserable.

We moved away before the end of the school year. I attended Churchill High School in Livonia, Michigan. By law, back then, a school was required to try to match the classes as closely as possible to your former school's class schedule. Here I was that nerdy freshman being tossed into a photography class full of seniors. I really felt out of place. Once again, I socially removed myself. I became so introverted that everything was upside-down in my world. I didn't want to connect with anyone. I never knew when the rug was going to be pulled out from under me again. I felt so insecure.

My photography teacher, Mr. Qualkenbush, or Mr. "Q" for short, was awesome. He must have been an introvert, too. He allowed me to work on my own, never forcing me into a group with these older strangers. In class, we had to copy images, make slides, and play them to music. I got an "A" on that "group" project. I might be showing my age, but that was way before PowerPoint and Animoto. I synced my project to the song "Rivendell" by Rush.

Looking back, I am amazed how aligned the lyrics were to where I was in my life at that time, and how they still relate to my life today. As an adult, I learned of Rivendell by Tolkien in the *Lord of the Rings* book trilogy.

It is a place in Middle-earth where the elves live. I do love fairies, but in high school, Tinker Bell was really the only fairy in my realm.

Those lyrics … "Sunlight dances through the leaves." The lyricist knew me. He knew how soft winds, warm grass, the sun on my face mirrored my emotions; the elven songs, endless nights. It was enchanting, haunting. I felt as if the song was meant for me. I could feel something calling, and me wanting to return to those misty mountains. I suggest you listen to the song yourself if you too are making an artistic journey, standing with your senses reeling, or are feeling out of place and alone in the world.

Fan the Flame

WHEN YOU THINK OF YOUR CREATIVE SELF, WHAT EXPERIENCES DO YOU RECALL AS MAKING YOU BELIEVE YOU ARE… OR AREN'T…A CREATIVE BEING?

IS BEING CREATIVE OR "MAKING ART" IMPORTANT TO YOU? WHY?

HOW HAVE JOY AND PAIN MIXED IN YOUR LIFE TO MAKE YOU WHO YOU ARE?

DO YOU THINK A PERSON CAN EXPERIENCE TRUE JOY IF SHE HASN'T EXPERIENCED EQUALLY POWERFUL PAIN?

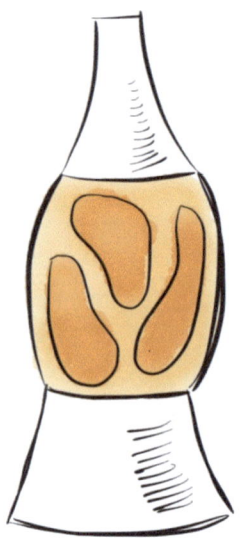

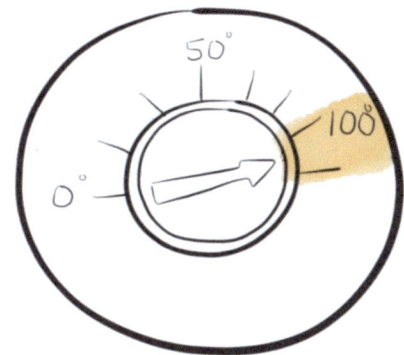

IT'S GETTING HOT IN HERE

I guess it was my crush on Derek Beach, a guy in my science class, that sparked my passion for portraiture. He loved the band Rush (now you see where I got my inspiration for my photography project), and was a drummer for a Led Zeppelin cover band that went to our school. I was so excited he said yes when I asked him to be the model for my portrait project. I was squealing and telling my girlfriend, not knowing he had turned back around to ask me a question and was standing right behind me. I was busted, damn it! I was a nervous wreck during the shoot, but now I had these fabulous pictures to gaze into his eyes anytime I wanted; plus, his mom loved them. I totally ROCKED it!

    Then my crushing ways shifted to another boy. Let's call him "Hot Thang." Hot Thang was in one of my classes and was on the track team, and I enjoyed shooting their practices. Since my math teacher was the coach, I couldn't wait to show him the pictures I took. He said, "These are great; now I can show Hot Thang what he is doing wrong in his broad jump." I was dying! Lesson learned: Being a photographer can provide some up-close-and-personal opportunities, but I didn't win any Brownie points with "Hot Thang" on this one.

Back to Mr. Q … he was also a graphic arts teacher, and he let me visit his class a few times during my free period. He taught me how to use the process camera and silk-screen equipment. I made a beautiful white silkscreen image of Kris Kristofferson on a black T-shirt. I thought he was so hot, even though at the time he was more than old enough to be my father. Daddy issues? Maybe. Probably. Of course.

Mr. Q's kind gesture would prove life-changing for me, and it set me on a career path that neither one of us could have anticipated. Being able to focus my attention on photography and graphic arts gave me a place to escape to when everything else in my life seemed so unpredictable.

"I totally ROCKED it!"

Fan the Flame

WHAT CRAFT, HOBBY OR WORK IN YOUR LIFE HAS SAVED YOU FROM SOME OF THE NOT-SO-FUN PARTS OF LIFE?

WHO IN YOUR LIFE HAS BEEN YOUR MENTOR WHEN YOU WERE LET DOWN BY THOSE WHO COULDN'T DO THE JOB?

HAVE YOU DISCOVERED THAT OPPORTUNITIES AFFORDED TO YOU BY OTHERS CHANGED YOUR LIFE'S PATH? HOW SO?

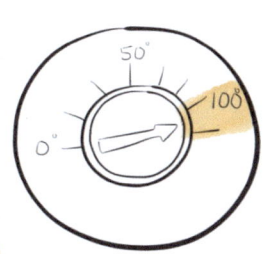

THE SLOW BURN
(I CALL IT 'HIGH SCHOOL')

My life took another turn when my mom and stepfather were having some marital problems. That initiated yet another move. This time, my brother and I were sent back to Florida. We were excited to go. "Finally!" we thought. We were each sent to live with a different aunt. I went to Aunt Jane and Uncle Bill, and he went to Aunt Mimi and Uncle Mike.

To say Aunt Jane and Uncle Bill were overprotective of me is an understatement. Uncle Bill wouldn't even let me mow the lawn because a rock might hit me. I so loved my Aunt Jane though. I always felt like she was my second-chance grandma, since my grandma died when I was 13. Our similarities became more obvious over the years. I can remember Aunt Jane and my mom commenting that perhaps Jane's daughter, Sue, and I might have been switched at birth. And sometimes I had to wonder.

In my sophomore year of high school, my creativity was focused on the school yearbook. I attended Stranahan High School in Ft. Lauderdale, Florida, and was on the yearbook staff. I found out years later that my layout designs were actually used for the yearbook. They titled it *Castles,*

Kings and Queens. But I never got to see the finished yearbook. I moved to my Aunt Mimi's house before it was completed.

I loved my Aunt Jane, but Uncle Bill got a little too friendly when he had too much to drink. My Aunt Mimi was closer to my mom's age and was the one who always had an eye out for my brother and me behind the scenes. I knew that if anything got really bad for us, she would step in.

I never felt like my brother J.R. or cousins Jenny and Jeff cared for me much. I was the youngest granddaughter and a real goody-two-shoes. I didn't smoke pot and rarely took aspirin. It didn't matter to me though. I didn't need their approval. I was grateful to be back "home." I was no longer isolated and alone, but I was still feeling lonely. I just tried to lay low and not be trouble for anyone.

This was my old neighborhood. I was transferred to South Plantation High School, which I would have attended had we never moved in the first place. I was back where I belonged … sort of.

I should have felt great, but I didn't. I felt awful. For so many years, my friends and I all anticipated going to "south," yet here I was lost, lonely and a total misfit. Not the perky cheerleader and homecoming queen who had left a few long years before.

The classes terrified me. I felt so unsettled and like I couldn't absorb anything into my brain. I didn't know where to turn or how to get help. I felt so stupid and certain I would fail.

Matching my schedule in each new school was not serving me well at all. When you attend five high schools, by the time you're at the fourth school, there are surely going to be gaps in your education. I know there are a lot of things I didn't learn that I should have learned in high school. It was all I could do to show up and make it through with a decent grade.

Did you ever have a dream where you had a test and were late for class and or you couldn't find your locker? My dream for years was going to my graduation ceremony and discovering all my credits didn't transfer and I didn't have enough to graduate. That one haunted me for years!

Before our first move, most of my neighborhood friends while I was growing up were boys. Now they were young men with hairy armpits, for God's sake! They all had girlfriends, and a life. I was no longer a part of things, and didn't fit in.

About two weeks after I moved in with Aunt Mimi, she got sick. It was the middle of the night when Uncle Mike took her to the hospital. She died the next day from cardiac arrest.

This was surreal. I became totally numb. My brother, cousins and I plotted to run away or hide so my mom couldn't make us move back to Michigan, but there was really no place else for us to go. I felt so bad leaving our cousins. This was so much loss at one time. My brother and I were hurting for them, and they were being protective and hurting for us.

It wasn't long after Aunt Mimi's funeral before my brother and I found ourselves back in Michigan. We didn't know what we would be facing when we got there, and we weren't really sure that anyone was happy or ready for our return.

I don't remember much discussion about what we had all been through when Aunt Mimi died. My mom had just lost her sister. I had just lost the person who was my safety net. But I had the inkling my stepfather may have liked a kid-free home better. My brother was always acting out and getting in some kind of trouble. I just tried to be good and be invisible. I figured my brother gave them enough to deal with. It didn't seem like much had changed, but it sure was hard to get back into the groove. I had a hard time adjusting. It was especially hard to reconnect with my friends, even my best friend. She now had new friends and a boyfriend. I was lost now. It felt like I was starting over again, and I knew it was just a matter of time before there would be another transfer, a new school and new friends to not fit in with.

When my brother and I returned to Michigan, I was in my junior year. One of my classes was Distributive Education Clubs of America. Of course I missed out on most of the curriculum, but arrived a few weeks before a competition. I remember two things about this experience: I came in second place for my merchandising display, and our class project was on creating a store. My store was called "Over the Rainbow." It's rather funny now that I look back on it. Maybe it was serendipitous. The items in the store were made by local high-school artists. I was always amazed by the incredible art projects that were on display from the students at our school. It seems that my shop today could have grown from that seed planted with a school project in 1978. That amazes me!

Soon enough, my stepfather was transferred to Oklahoma. We were on the road again. I remember my parents going ahead of us to check out the area. My mom was so excited to tell me I would be going to Moore High School because the school mascot was a lion. I am a Leo and collected lions back then. As thrilled as I was about the mascot, I was a little more than concerned about whether the roads were paved in Oklahoma, and if everyone looked like cowboys and Indians there.

Now in Oklahoma, I was finishing up my junior year and a few months before the summer break, a pamphlet came in the mail from the local vo-tech school. All the classes listed there looked pretty interesting. Then, there it was, Graphic Arts! I thought, *"Way cool, I can make T-shirts all*

> "Inside I breathed a sigh of relief when I realized that just maybe I wouldn't have to Baby-sit or serve burgers as a career for the rest of my life."

summer long!" I was hoping that summer would give me some time to meet other kids, make friends, and get to know more about our new community. I didn't want to feel so raw and vulnerable walking into classes in the fall my senior year.

As I quickly learned, there was a lot more to graphic arts than I ever knew. There was so much to learn. It was exhilarating and nerve-racking all at the same time. I started with the darkroom, which I thought would be a great fit. I loved photography. But in this darkroom almost all the principles were the reverse from photography as I knew it. Still, I found the challenge to be fun.

By the end of the summer, I had the darkroom down and was running a printing press taller than myself. I loved what I had experienced so far. I enrolled in the fall program, and my hard work paid off as I was able to graduate from this two-year program with my certification in printing and graphic arts by the end of my senior year. I learned every aspect of pre-press and printing except typesetting; that would come later. My instructor, Mr. Johnson, encouraged me to compete in a Vocational Industrial Clubs of America event. I placed second in the county and the region. Inside, I breathed a sigh of relief when I realized that just maybe I wouldn't have to baby-sit or serve burgers as a career for the rest of my life.

Fan the Flame

THINK BACK TO A TIME WHEN EVENTS LINED UP TO CREATE A NEW REALITY FOR YOU, EVEN WHEN YOU DIDN'T KNOW IT AT THE TIME.

HOW WERE YOU SURPRISED AT HOW THINGS TURNED OUT?

WHEN THE PATH WAS MOST UNCERTAIN, WHAT KEPT YOU GOING? WHO KEPT YOU GOING?

HAVE YOU THANKED THEM?

WOO HOO! I'M EMPLOYABLE!
(THAT'S A GOOD THING, I THINK.)

After high-school graduation, I was working for Hertz Reservation Center in Oklahoma City. Once my supervisor found out that my stepfather worked for another rental-car agency, they terminated my employment for fear of industrial espionage. When someone explained what that was to me, it sounded ridiculous. I was thinking, *"I just graduated from high school; they think I'm a spy?"* My stepfather and I were not on the greatest terms at the time, but the Universe was looking out for me. Not only did this whole job fiasco bring us closer, my stepfather stepped up and did everything in his power to fix it. He found me another job. He did that for me. I started working at the airport for National Car Rental next, and thankfully they didn't care who my daddy worked for.

One day, I received a surprise phone call from Mr. Johnson at vo-tech. He asked if I was working and if I was happy and working in my *field*. It turns out Mr. Johnson belonged to a printing association. One of the members was looking to hire someone. He thought of me. I got the job working at a print shop and was like a sponge absorbing everything I could.

> "Every job from there was like a stepping stone in my life."

Every job from there was like a stepping stone in my life. I built up skill after skill, adding another tool to my toolbox with each one. I found myself working in a commercial print shop doing typesetting and layout, and I remember when Mac's Apple computer hit our office. As a typesetter, I found it amazing that you could actually see what you were creating on the screen instead of typing in code.

One of the best places I ever worked was the Solid Waste Authority of Palm Beach County. I was back in Florida and worked there for almost eight years. I held five different positions ranging from data-entry clerk and graphic specialist to volunteer coordinator.

Afterward, I went on to work for the School District of Palm Beach County as area volunteer coordinator, and then was recruited by Communities in Schools to recruit and train mentors for the Take Stock in Children program. I was then solicited by the Children's Services Council of Palm Beach County to manage and supervise the administrative team for the agency. I had volunteered at my church, Unity of the Palm Beaches leading their marketing team and was eventually hired as their director of operations. Even in positions that were typically analytical, I could always bring a creative spin and exceed expectations.

It was actually one of the young women I supervised who told me about the Disney cartoon *Kim Possible*. I loved the idea of having a powerful and positive nickname (I am woman! Hear me roar!). The nickname has stuck with me ever since.

Looking back, it all seems kind of amazing. I'm realizing that when we connect and become a part of community, we increase the flow for opportunity, growth and accomplishments. In 2006, after 18 years in South Florida, I flipped a coin and made the decision to move to Central Florida.

Fan the Flame

WHAT ARE YOUR MOST POWERFUL PERSONALITY TRAITS THAT LEAD TO YOUR SUCCESS?

WHAT TALENTS AND SKILLS COME EASILY TO YOU?

ARE YOU COMFORTABLE TELLING PEOPLE WHO YOU ARE, AND WHAT MAKES YOU SUCCESSFUL?

IS CONNECTIVITY IMPORTANT TO YOU AT WORK? WHY?

WHERE THERE'S SMOKE, THERE'S 'FIRED'

When the Artist's Way group concluded, the Tribe continued to meet. We took turns and met at someone's house, ate, drank, and did a creative project together. Since I was part of this Tribe, I decided if I wanted to call myself an artist, I should at the very least be a part of this Women's Museum I had just discovered. I became a member and met with Crystal, the executive director, about volunteer opportunities. I don't just join anything; I become *engaged!*

One day, I noticed that there was a "rent me" sign downstairs from the museum. I hadn't noticed it before. *"What a great location for a party or event,"* I thought. I had heard the museum rented the space for events. Maybe the Tribe could put something creative together. So, once again I met with Crystal, and we discussed the space. What the museum was really looking for was to have someone lease the space for long-term use. There were a variety of business prospects; however, it was the museum's hope to have an art-related business enter the space. Crystal told me about an artist co-op that used to exist, and we brainstormed the possibilities.

That meeting was on Oct. 5, 2012, and my head was spinning. I reached out via email to 25 creative women that I knew to see if they or someone they knew might be interested in being a part of a retail space to promote their work. I tossed out a few ideas about costs and splits; and only mentioned it would be a prominent location in downtown DeLand. I got a really good response, and then, wait for it … I did nothing. I love capturing an idea, making plans, and developing processes, but I lacked the motivation to move forward.

Three days later, I had awful stomach pains after a late lunch, and Michael picked me up from work and took me to the emergency room. I begged him not to take me. I said, "They are just going to see a fat woman, tell me I have gas, and send me home." Thank God on this day Michael ignored me and probably saved my life. Later that night, I was diagnosed with acute pancreatitis.

While I healed a bit in the ER, they gave me morphine to help relieve the pain, and that worked for all of about 15 minutes. I was in a lot of pain, extremely nauseated and vomiting. By the time I was admitted, the nurse and I discussed options for relief. She had something that might have helped me, but she hesitated because it tends to make patients nauseated, and I was already so sick. We decided I would ride it out for the night.

In the morning, I said I was ready for anything. Oh, dear God, the agony! They shot me with something, and I felt a wave throughout my body that took away the pain. I wondered, *"Why the heck was I trying to be so tough?"* And exactly four hours later, my body knew it was time for another dose, and it became very clear to me how people could get addicted to drugs. That was some good stuff, I tell you; I can't remember what it was, and I don't want to know. The lesson here: There is nothing proud or honorable about suffering. If someone offers you help, take it. You don't have to prove anything to anybody.

Four days later, my gallbladder was removed, and I was released from the hospital a few days after that. When I got home, I found an email and phone message from Crystal following up to see if I was going to submit a proposal to lease the space at the Women's Museum. She had shared our conversation with a board member, who in turn brought it up at their meeting, and the board was interested in seeing a proposal. I explained to Crystal that I had been in the hospital and her call inspired me to take the next step. Up to this point, this was just a *wouldn't this be cool to do someday* kind of idea.

So another email went out to the same 25 women, letting them know I was going to write a proposal. I started planning, deciding on a name, creating a logo, and setting up the Facebook page and website. I did anything I could think of to have everything secure and in place for the one day I might have the guts to make this happen. I was getting excited.

Both Michael, who is totally amazing and incredibly supportive, and my mother, who had retail experience, provided checks and balances so I wasn't totally jumping off the deep end. Michael hadn't worked for several months, so I thought I could create the road map and then he and Mom could work at the shop. I could have some fun and work at the shop in the evenings and on weekends. Sounds like a great plan, right? After I was working all day long in a stressful and somewhat hostile work environment, I could just pop into the shop. I have to admit, my plans and ideas may not always be based in other people's reality, and that is OK, as long as I feel it is possible, I will make it happen.

> "Nothing was making sense. It took me a few minutes to realize what was going on; I was being fired from my job."

A week after my gallbladder surgery, I was cleared from the doctor to go back to work. I think the time I spent away from the office slowed me down enough for me to realize I hated my job. I was doing my very best to stay positive. I was a taskmaster who made many improvements, but the thought of going back to that office was depressing; it was all I could do to get out of bed, get dressed, apply some makeup, and get myself to the office.

I came in the back door, and yelled, "Good morning." No response. I thought maybe my boss was on the phone, but as I approached her office door, I could see someone was in there. "Oh, geez," I thought, "She's in a meeting." She called me into her office and introduced the visitor as someone from the company that provided our human resource services and benefits. She asked me to sit down.

Nothing was making sense. It took me a few minutes to realize what was going on; I was being fired from my job. On top of that, I was being falsely accused of wrongdoing. I started to explain. I wanted to clarify the misunderstanding. Then it hit me, I was being fired from a job I didn't like.

There was really nothing more to discuss. I was asked to pack up my personal items and made my exit. Thank goodness. What a relief. My inner voice was kicking my butt. "You should have listened," it said. I called Michael and told him, "Don't leave; I was just fired and I am on my way home." I was angry, humiliated, shocked and devastated. I worked hard at that job. To me, getting fired felt completely and utterly personal.

Fan the Flame

HAS THERE BEEN A TIME WHEN YOU WERE RESISTANT TO OTHERS' HELP? WHAT WAS THE LESSON YOU LEARNED? OR, ARE YOU STILL WORKING ON IT?

REJECTION IS A HUGE FEAR MOST OF US HOLD. HOW HAVE YOU REACTED IN THE FACE OF REJECTION? WOULD YOU REACT DIFFERENTLY IF THAT REJECTION HAPPENED TODAY?

WHO HAVE YOU REJECTED? HOW DID THEY REACT? WOULD YOU HAVE HANDLED THE SITUATION DIFFERENTLY?

OUT OF HELL, AND INTO A HOT 'TRUNK'

In any case, it was the push I needed; I did not have the courage to leave on my own. I left carrying a small cardboard box to my car, feeling a roller coaster of emotions all the way home. Once again, the Universe took care of what I couldn't do for myself. I was taken totally by surprise.

When I got home, Michael met me on our front steps. I was in tears, and told him I had been totally miserable at my job but in no way had I tried to get fired. He said in his adorable British accent, "I know."

Once the initial shock wore off and I was able to talk with Michael, I thought it was the funniest damn thing ever, and I felt like a ton of bricks had been lifted off my shoulders. And when I asked Michael, "What are we going to do?" he said, "We're going to open that shop, Funky Trunk Treasures."

When I started getting my ducks in a row to open Funky Trunk, I was so excited, because I love creating and developing projects, programs, and plans. I was wondering to myself, *Will this work? Will they let me do it?* I didn't even know who "they" were; I just kept moving forward thinking, *"I'll just keep going until I hit a brick wall, and if it is meant to be, it will be."* The Universe had set me free, and I was going to ride this wave as far as it would take me.

Funky Trunk Treasures was about to become a reality. This retail space would be filled with items from local artists and artisans for a unique shopping experience, and we would offer classes and workshops for people like me who wanted to learn and play, but not invest in every craft project that caught their eye. We would have classes for personal, professional, and creative development.

The lease was signed and the deal was sealed on Nov. 9, 2012. It was now official, and we had subleased a space from the Women's Museum in the heart of downtown DeLand. Now what? I thought for sure someone would have stopped me by now, or laughed at me and asked, *"Who do you think you are?"* I had only been in this community for six years; how well did anyone really know me? This DeLand thing was new territory for me, and it seemed like a hard nut to crack.

The Women's Museum was such a blessing for me. I wanted them as much as they wanted me. What I wasn't aware of were the challenges and financial struggles they were having when I signed my lease. And you know what? I am most thankful for that. If I had known, I would have never had the courage to take the leap of faith wondering about the "what if's." Even though the museum catered more to fine art and we were more artisans, Crystal and many of their members and volunteers embraced our presence. The Women's Museum was leasing their space from the City of DeLand and so the advantage of subleasing was that it was fast and easy, but on the other hand, it left me vulnerable.

> "The Universe had set me free, and I was going to ride this wave as far as it would take me."

Fan the Flame

HAS THE SUPPORT OF A LOVED ONE EVER CATAPULTED YOU TO TAKE A RISK?

HOW DID IT TURN OUT?

WHY DO YOU TAKE RISKS?

RISKING HAS COSTS, TOO. ARE THEY WORTH IT, IN YOUR EXPERIENCE? WHY?

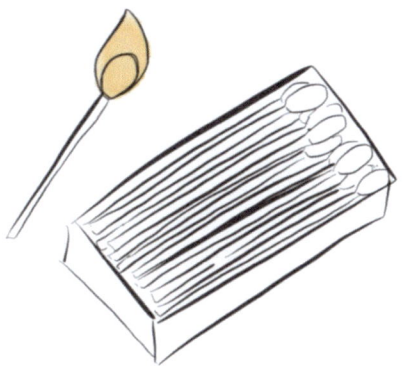

RAPID-FIRE CHANGE: THE FUNKY TRUNK COMBUSTION

Funky Trunk Treasures opened on Black Friday, just two weeks after we signed our lease. We had 25 artists on board when we opened our doors. It wasn't long before word spread and we were approached almost daily by artists wanting to bring in their work. I was so excited, hoping that we would have enough artists to fill up our 1,900 square feet of space. I felt honored these talented people would consider being part of Funky Trunk.

It wasn't long before I noticed many artists seemed nervous when they came in. They were nervous about whether they'd be "chosen" to have their goods sold in my shop. I never expected that reaction. In my mind, we needed each other. I saw this as a partnership, not a competition. I still feel that way today.

It's interesting how we see ourselves, isn't it? Our self-perception is usually nowhere close to how others view us. In the past, my experience has always been that others see more in me than I see in myself. Now here come these artists, testing the waters, hoping they would have a place to display and sell their creations and a spot to be introduced into the world.

> "It's interesting how we see ourselves, isn't it? Our perception is usually nowhere close to how others view us."

To help alleviate nerves, I asked each artist to fill out an application; then I would make an appointment and talk with each one-on-one. No matter what the circumstances or personality, I could always see an aspect of myself in each artist. I felt very connected to them. I had struggled to see myself as an artist, and I wanted validation for my craft. In turn, I hoped I could not only provide a venue for the artists' work, but a place where they could get that validation and a place where they could possibly see themselves and their talent more clearly. No matter how an artist comes across, how confident we are on the outside, we all need some type of validation; someone to say our work is valuable. It took me a while to realize that, because I had my own insecurities to deal with.

Some of the statements I heard many times over were, "Oh, I really don't care about making money; I just want to keep doing what I love and recoup some money for supplies." And, "I want to mark the price low enough so people will buy it." I was catapulted smack-dab in the middle of being a coach and mentor. I may have had those same thoughts and feelings myself, but they sounded so crazy coming out of someone else's mouth. *"I'm not a real artist, but if people buy my stuff that means my work is good."* There are obviously much bigger issues at play here. There was and is always something much deeper revealed once you scratch the surface on any type of talent. We really don't know what is in someone's heart or what may be holding them back.

Within three months, I had 75 artist partners at Funky Trunk Treasures — whew, how did that happen? I was clueless about being a merchant. Talk about a confidence issue. I felt I didn't really know what I was doing. I had never done anything like this before. Me? I'm not boss material. I just kept showing up every day, and did the next thing that had to be done. There wasn't much time to doubt or whine, just do what I could do to keep the balls in the air.

A very valuable thing I learned about myself is, I didn't know how to say no. Sure, I had almost daily opportunities to learn and grow, and I was learning more about retail business, but I was also diving deep into the black hole. Where was I going? I really wanted to have a positive business give my customers a positive shopping experience, but I was the one calling all the shots here. The buck stopped with me. I can remember so many times at other jobs, working on teams and with committees. I would sometimes become impatient with the process; *"Let's just make a decision already and move on."* How I wish I had a team to help make decisions now. My brain was feeling overloaded. Could I really do this? I had to. These artists were depending on me.

I felt protective of my "new baby." I think most new business owners do. I had something in mind. I hated when someone came in with a holier-than-thou attitude about their work, or made comments about someone else's artwork that wasn't welcomed at my place. I knew I didn't want negativity growing in my shop. This was Funky Trunk, the place with a big comfortable couch where everyone was welcome.

I find attitude can be connected to insecurities, so I usually give people the benefit of the doubt until they prove me wrong two or three times. Sometimes people just need support; a hug, someone to believe in them. Other times, people have been carrying so much baggage around for so long they are more comfortable holding the weight. They're used to carrying it around all the time and talking about it to others. Change would be a strange concept to them. When I couldn't shake the negativity, well … "You gotta know when to hold 'em, know when to fold 'em." (Thanks, Kenny!) You don't have to say yes to everyone; just let them walk away.

Fan the Flame

DO YOU RECOGNIZE YOURSELF IN ANY OF THESE ARTISTS?

DO YOU FIND YOURSELF JUDGING THEIR FEELINGS, FEELING COMPASSIONATE ABOUT THEIR STRUGGLES OR INDIFFERENT? WHY?

HOW HAS LEARNING ABOUT OTHERS' HANG-UPS, SENSITIVITIES AND EMOTIONAL NEEDS HELPED YOU UNDERSTAND YOURSELF BETTER?

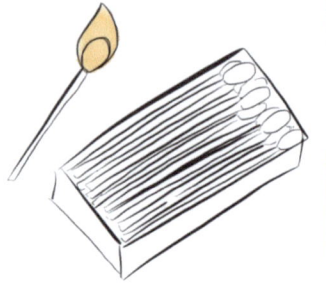

THERE SHE IS AGAIN: THE INNER VOICE SPEAKETH

It took about a year, and a move to a new location, for me to really get my business bearings. In that period of time, I met a variety of artists with a wide range of experiences and energy. I began to realize while I was so consumed with the needs of others and their feelings, I was disregarding my needs and feelings.

If I stayed on this path, I would not be able to stay in business or attract the artists I wanted and enough customers to sustain the shop. It was time to do some soul-searching and really decide what kind of life and what kind of business I really wanted to create.

One artist who came along was attractive, had retail experience, and a lot of energy. My heart felt for her because clearly her intentions were genuine. As I got to know her, I saw a part of myself in her. It was a part of myself I didn't like, but I could relate to it. She had too much energy. It was overwhelming. I began to wonder how my energy might have overwhelmed people I had worked with in the past. Did I make them feel discounted and uncomfortable?

This artist and I eventually parted ways. This brings me to another lesson. I learned that no matter how good your intentions are or how big your heart is, sometimes associations may not be a good fit. People are in our lives for a reason or a season. Take it for what it is, and let it go.

Another artist who came in really had me feeling anxious. I found I was uncomfortable with her. She is excellent at what she does, and she sells items in other shops. There was no logical reason for me to be nervous around her. I felt intimidated. Then I thought about it. How many times have I made other people feel intimidated without realizing it? Take note, learning about being in business for yourself can also be an adventure of self-exploration. I was still learning the ropes of my business, and I had plenty of growing pains yet to come. It took me a long time to feel comfortable around this artist, but she has consistently remained one of my sellers and producers. Sometimes all it takes is a shift in your perception. I appreciate her and the work she does. I learned that it's business; we don't have to take vacations together.

I met an artist, Tracey (she did the illustrations in this book!), in the first Artist's Way group I facilitated at Funky Trunk. Tracey is beautiful inside and out. It is no coincidence that I immediately felt a kinship with her since we both share a Unity Church connection. When I saw her Zentangle-inspired art, I was in awe. Her creations reflected her so beautifully. I couldn't understand why she wasn't selling her work other places or teaching somewhere. It was not her goal to be rich. She wanted to create and distribute and learn to say yes to the possibilities. Here comes another lesson. I learned that knowing your intentions and honoring the process along the way are key to not only creating, but to increasing the flow to our individual highest good.

> "We must always be responsible for our actions and how we treat others."

One afternoon, a perky little artist came in, and she became part of Funky Trunk Treasures. She possessed a great attitude, and was very creative. I could immediately relate to her. Like me, she is all over the place. She is good at so many things. She just didn't know where to focus. If you like doing a lot of things and you're good at a lot of things, it is hard to narrow down the scope. What I have noticed in others and now see more clearly in myself is, when I try to do it all it is really hard to see what I am passionate about and what makes my heart sing. We are so busy putting it all out there to see what sticks, that we no longer feel creative or joyful. If we can get real and tap into what fills us with joy and trust, everything does seem to fall into place.

When I was younger, friendships in the workplace were frowned upon, discouraged, or even forbidden. I have had some of the best friendships from people I met through my jobs. As a business owner, I am so eager to help others, I don't always think situations all the way through. This can make me an easy target for people to take advantage of my generosity, making me vulnerable and feeling foolish. It has happened with an artist or two, and it is incredibly painful when I discover someone has not been honest with me or someone lacks integrity. Personally, this heartache has been the hardest for me to overcome. Apparently I have a very sensitive and trusting nature. It's something I like about myself and admire in others, but isn't always practical. When it happens and I get burned, I have to forgive myself for being and feeling so foolish; then I can be grateful that I have a prosperous heart and move on.

I have seen patterns over time. From observation, I can tell when artists stop communicating and/or their sales slow down, their focus and energy are somewhere else. It's all part of the ebb and flow of the business.

It's not personal. Since I am the queen of taking things personally, I really do need to release and let go. Again, it's not personal. A part of me does feel sad whenever an artist leaves, no matter what the reason — I am definitely a work in progress.

Fan the Flame

HOW ARE SOME OF THE ASPECTS OF YOUR PERSONALITY BOTH HELPFUL AND HARMFUL TO YOUR RELATIONSHIPS WITH OTHERS?

IS IT POSSIBLE THAT SOMETHING ABOUT YOU CAN HELP AND HINDER YOUR RELATIONSHIPS SIMULTANEOUSLY?

HAVE YOU EVER TAKEN ANYTHING TOO PERSONALLY? WHY?

THE CONTROLLED BURN: SETTING PARAMETERS FOR MY BUSINESS

There is one situation that remains consistent. People will visit the shop and inquire about how artists become a part of Funky Trunk Treasures. They have a friend, a daughter, or someone they know who would be perfect. They can see that person's artwork on my walls. That never pans out. When an artist is ready to put their artwork out there, they are ready. We can't want it for them or will them to do so. Seems like that scenario is true in a lot of cases in our lives.

I've also noticed that many artists have such a lack mentality that they assume they cannot afford to do the shop's standard consignment split even before they know what the retail price would be. I think they might feel a little scared or intimidated, and some people want to buy in to that whole starving artist thing. I don't know sometimes if it is an excuse, a mindset, or both. The clarifying question I have posed to many artists is, "Is it a business or a hobby?" Once that becomes clear, then our thoughts and actions will support whatever we think.

"Is it a business or a hobby?"

Fan the Flame

THINK OF A SITUATION WHEN SOMEONE YOU WANTED TO DO BUSINESS WITH HAD RULES YOU DIDN'T AGREE WITH.

DID YOU CHANGE YOUR MIND ABOUT THEM EVENTUALLY OR HOLD FIRM?

HOW IMPORTANT ARE RULES AND PARAMETERS IN BUSINESS?

HOW OFTEN DO YOU CHANGE YOUR MIND? DO YOU THINK THAT'S A STRONG QUALITY OR A WEAKNESS?

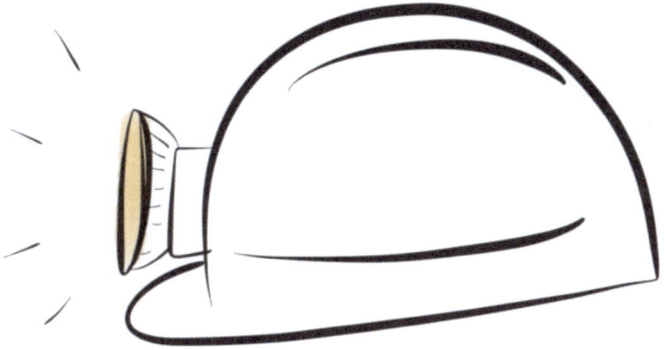

LEADERS CAN STAND THE HEAT, SO WHY AM I SO CHILLY?

I was introduced to the local merchants association before I became a merchant. Once I opened my shop, I joined. I felt that it was the only organization that came close to connecting businesses downtown. I was intimidated as hell, but I still attended the monthly meetings. The greatest benefit to these meetings for me was the chance to meet other business owners and put some names, faces and businesses together. In my mind, they all held the secret, the brotherhood of the merchants, and I didn't think that I would ever fit in.

    I kept thinking, *"They don't want me here; I'm funky; I'm an impostor, I don't belong here."* I was preoccupied with what their opinions of me were. I felt like I needed everyone's approval and acceptance. I just needed some indication that I was doing something, anything right. Because of my experience, I try to make a better effort to connect with new merchants. I remember all too well how it felt being the new kid on the block, downtown and in school.

> "They do not feel the need to be everything to everybody."

One merchant stood out as the most intimidating to me. She owned a "gallery." She has a direct communication style that I like, but it took me a while to catch her in a smile. Funky Trunk Treasures was my whole life. It didn't dawn on me that people had a life outside of being a merchant. *"Hello, Kim, it's not all about you. Don't take it personally."* Funny how I just assumed she didn't like me, or thought my shop was ridiculous. Today, she is one of my favorite merchants on the boulevard. She is funny, witty, smart, compassionate, a confidante and friend. I am so thankful for our relationship. She has given me so much support and encouragement.

It's easy to come in new and green, full of fire and energy, and question or judge what fellow merchants are doing. So many of the men and women who own these businesses have been operating them for a long time. They have found their groove and know what they can and can't do, and apparently it works for them. They do not feel the need to be everything to everybody, like I did. I may not be on the same page as some, but I respect them all. There is certainly nothing glamorous about being a downtown merchant. Not sure why I love it so much.

I've never been the type of person to just join something; I get engaged. I joined a committee and, eventually, was in charge. Here, like with my marriages, I stepped right in and was going to fix everything and make it all better. The committee seemed like a great place for me to be of service. I thought, *"I'm a merchant and I have plenty of artists to engage, and I have some mad skills; this should be a piece of cake."*

It wasn't long before I began to understand more about working with artists and merchants. It was literally like herding cats. Merchants are pulled in so many directions. They lack time and resources. Artists for the most part are sensitive souls who usually have way more creativity than they do business skills. This showed me that sometimes things don't need to be fixed, that, sometimes, life or events just evolve and there is a season and a reason for everything.

On the other hand, a monthly women's event is a different story. For the first six years I lived here, I rarely came downtown, and when I did, I was amazed at what I discovered. We've got it all here; the good, the bad and the ugly—a real eclectic mix. I felt pretty silly that we had so much to offer and I had always driven through our little downtown, but never really took the time to discover all it had to offer. This event would be the perfect opportunity for women, who, for whatever reason, like me never took the time to come downtown on the weekend and couldn't make it to venture out before shops closed during the week.

When I went to the association with my written proposal for this new event, it was a big step for me. The executive director was still fairly new to the job and getting his feet wet. I got the feeling he wasn't sure what to make of me. No one really knew about my experience and what I could bring to the table. Getting this reoccurring event approved finally made me feel like I was a part of something downtown.

Fan the Flame

HOW OFTEN DO YOU GET INTIMIDATED BY OTHERS' SUCCESS, POSSESSIONS OR PERSONALITY?

DO YOU OFTEN CREATE STORIES IN YOUR MIND ABOUT PEOPLE'S LIVES?

HOW DOES THIS SERVE YOU, OR DOES IT?

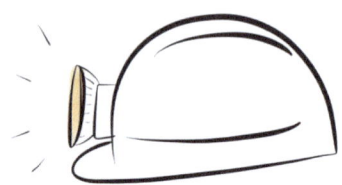

GIVING MYSELF PERMISSION: IT'S TIME TO MOVE

I have always heard that the first couple of years are toughest in business and in marriage. In business, don't expect to make any money and don't hate your business when you don't. I have also heard that many people give up right before the breakthrough, before they find success. I kept telling myself, *"I can't do this, we can't afford this, and how is this going to work?"* I was always feeling like I had no right to call myself a "creativity director," a title I gave myself as owner of my shop.

To complicate matters just a bit, right before Funky Trunk Treasures' one-year anniversary, I was presented with a new lease from a new landlord (same location). It left me sick to my stomach. There were changes I wasn't keen on. As soon as I signed the lease, for example, my street sign would have to come down. I would also lose my ability to be creative to the point that my landlord would have to "approve" my window display. Michael was out of the country at the time. When I contacted him, he said, "Let's move the shop." What? I just got uncomfortable there. I practically scolded him, listing all the reasons why we just couldn't do that. We had planned a business and opened it within seven weeks. I couldn't even grasp the idea of moving to another location. But the power of the new lease was too much for me. Ultimately, we made the decision to move the shop a few blocks north of the current location.

I was sharing my feelings of anxiety with Tracey. She always keeps it simple and goes right to the core of the issue. "You know, Kim," she said. "Funky Trunk is not about these four walls; it's about what you bring to it." I looked at her in amazement for a moment and said, "You mean I can move my shop?" "Yes," she said. "You have permission."

Wow, did that change things for me. I actually had permission. I could decide what I wanted to do. I felt so empowered. Immediately, I followed up with a merchant I had spoken with just a few weeks earlier. She was telling me about a space available to lease at the end of her block. (You know, if I was ever interested in moving.) At the time, moving was the furthest thing from my mind. But this new lease had me feeling like I was going to work with a pit in my stomach. I'd been there, done that — and I didn't want to relive it, thankyouverymuch. As a small-business owner, giving up my power to someone else certainly wasn't what I signed up for, I didn't sign the new lease.

When I met with my prospective new landlord, Don, and walked into the new space, it was love at first sight. Not with him, but with the space. I mean, he was super-nice, but there was a stage and two beautiful brick walls. It felt warm and inviting! I was home. My artists would be at home there. My customers would feel comfortable there. The space was previously a comedy club, and even today I sometimes tell customers it still is … depending upon who's working. (Ba-dum-bump!)

I felt so comfortable talking to Don, too. He was personable and professional. Everything felt so right. I really didn't want to push my luck, but I did ask Don if he would take $5 a month off the rent. That way, I could feel I did my due diligence to negotiate a better price. We both laughed, and he agreed. I knew I liked this guy. The awful feeling in my stomach vanished. I couldn't wait to move my shop to this beautiful new space.

I'll admit, as excited as I was, I was also scared out of my mind and a nervous wreck. There was so much to do. Looking back, I didn't realize everything I was capable of accomplishing. We only had two-and-a-half weeks to orchestrate the move. Don and I only had an oral agreement to start (that's trust), and we signed the lease about three weeks later on a Wednesday afternoon. Then, the keys were mine.

On the following Friday afternoon, a friend started painting walls. The carpets had been cleaned, and we started moving in the bigger pieces of furniture that night. We continued working in shifts over the next couple of days. To my delight, all the artists pitched in. We never missed a beat. We kept the old location open during the move, and we opened the new location on Tuesday morning. It was like Funky Trunk had been there the entire time.

It's hard to believe, but we did that very physical move in only four days without a hitch. I know this seems a little wacky, but this is how I roll! This was such a great lesson about trust and letting go for me. I had done it with a team of artists who believed in me and Funky Trunk Treasures. One year earlier, I would not have had the courage to pull it off.

Being a downtown merchant, I have met so many incredible business men and women. When I moved to my current location, complete

"Wow, did that change things for me. I had permission. I could decide what I wanted to do. I felt so empowered."

with its kind landlord and brick walls, the merchants on the block really embraced me. I am forever grateful to them, and enjoy their support and camaraderie.

Moving the shop was certainly in the highest good for all concerned. I have the best landlord and an amazing space that exudes warmth and creativity. Even though I was terrified when it happened, I do believe the Universe was acting on my behalf and working to get my attention once again. My inner voice was cheering me on.

Fan the Flame

IS IT TIME YOU GAVE YOURSELF PERMISSION TO MAKE A CHANGE IN YOUR LIFE?

HOW DOES THAT CHANGE CAUSE YOU FEAR, DOUBT OR UNCERTAINTY?

IF SOMEONE IN YOUR LIFE WERE TO GIVE YOU PERMISSION, WOULD THAT MAKE THE CHANGE EASIER TO EMBRACE? WHY?

MOVING MY SHOP CHALLENGED ME TO TRUST AND LET GO. WHAT IN YOUR LIFE DO YOU NEED TO CHANGE IN ORDER FOR YOU TO DO THE SAME?

I AM PROSPEROUS – DARN IT!

Heading into the next holiday season, Funky Trunk Treasures' sales almost doubled! I was thrilled, obviously. But hanging out there were tales of woes from other merchants about how bad things were in the summer on our little Main Street. These tales echoed in my mind. I would say to myself, "*I choose for that not to be my experience.*" I'll admit it's not the best affirmation, if you think about it. Affirmations should affirm what we desire, not what we don't want to happen. I often go to my old standby, my personal affirmation, "*I am prosperous!*" but that has to do with a lot more than just money. During the winter months and into spring, I continued to work harder, fine-tune every process, look to see what was working, and what was missing, all while working seven days a week.

I found myself so stressed out and exhausted that my thoughts ran wild daily. As good as things were going, cash flow was unpredictable at the shop. Michael was working again (thank God), and anything left over after paying our personal bills was being put into Funky Trunk.

> "Some decisions were costly, and some bruised the crap out of my ego."

I am always amazed at Michael's undying support. I love that man! We had been financially feeding Funky Trunk Treasures every month. I wasn't sure if or when I would see light at the end of the tunnel. I often thought, *"How long before enough is enough? Do I go on? Do I cut my losses and close the shop? Am I crazy? Who do I think I am? I don't know what I'm doing!"* I struggled to let go of my self-imposed perfectionism and just kept doing my best. Even so, I would beat myself up when a bill was late. All the time, I was believing everyone else has this "small-business retail model" figured out. Where was this model no one had shared with me? I didn't get that memo. They all understood it, I thought. Everyone but me.

Not only was I stressed out financially, I was rarely taking time off. On top of that, I wasn't getting paid! Michael, as sweet, loving, and supportive as he is, has said to me on more than one occasion, "You're not a good businessperson because you follow your heart too much." His remark cut me like a knife. His opinion of me matters most in this world. There he was with his stern, logical, British accent. I felt like I was scolded for having those nasty little things called "feelings." Of course, I only heard that I am not a good businessperson, not that I have too much heart. And in hindsight, many decisions could have been easier if I had stepped out of my emotions to see things more clearly. Some of my emotional decisions were costly, and some bruised the hell out of my ego.

Most people who meet me pick up on my Leo personality and assume I am an extrovert and tough as nails. Lord knows I can be very direct. However, it's the people who love me and know me best who know what a sensitive lioness I really am. The flip side of that big personality is my Scorpio moon and rising; it's my introvert side, always struggling to just go somewhere alone to hide and lick my wounds. I'm certain a decadent siesta wouldn't hurt either.

Fan the Flame

WHAT IS YOUR GO-TO MANTRA WHEN YOU NEED TO CALM YOURSELF? UNDER WHAT CIRCUMSTANCES DO YOU FIND YOURSELF RECITING IT?

WE ARE ALL EMOTIONAL BEINGS, BUT SOME OF US ARE MORE COMPLICATED THAN OTHERS. WHAT DO YOU DO WHEN YOU FEEL CONFLICTED ABOUT A DECISION YOU'VE MADE OR SITUATION YOU FACE?

DOES YOUR EMOTIONAL OR LOGICAL SELF TAKE THE LEAD?

DO YOU FEEL ABUNDANT? WHAT MAKES YOU FEEL THAT WAY?

LET THAT FLAME GROW TALLER, LADIES!

You know how men love to solve problems and rescue, right? Well, over the summer, after our second year running Funky Trunk, Michael suggested we sell our house and move in with my mother so I could have additional revenue to support Funky Trunk. I almost fell over. I thought this was such a sweet, loving gesture. This man is so supportive … is he out of his effing mind? I didn't know whether to laugh or cry at his proposal to move in with Mom, nor which scared me more, leaving the home we created together or living with my mother.

Don't get me wrong, my mom is one of the most amazing women I know. She's funny, smart, creative, and she loves me. But moving home to Momma just screamed failure to me. I called my mom thinking we could both have a laugh about Michael's idea. I was surprised to hear that she agreed with Michael as she shared how it could benefit her, too.

Regardless of everyone else's suggestions and opinions on the move, I was a bit upset and stressed about all of this. Such feelings, thankfully, usually lead me to suck it up and "put on my big-girl panties."

> "Finally, all the struggles and lessons I learned paid off. I was now able to stand up and speak my truth without fear."

So, the day after the ideas had been floated, I created a personal budget and a business budget, researched property values, and was ready to present them to Michael that evening. We sat down, and I presented my case as to why selling our home was not a good idea.

I knew there was some merit to his suggestion, but I felt proud presenting my case. This was a big step for me. In the past, I wouldn't step up to state my side of an issue. I felt everyone knew more than I did and I should just go along for the ride. I was a business woman now, growing and learning. I figured my decisions should count for something. Here I was, calm and collected, explaining my points.

When it was all said and done, Michael and I made the decision to rent our home out. We would divert any needed funds from that revenue for the business and, yes, we moved in with my mom, "Crazy Carol." Thanks, Mom!

As we finished up our conversation, I revisited Michael's comments that had hurt me, how he said I'm not a good businessperson because I follow my heart too much. I very calmly and clearly told him that I was new to this business world and that nothing, no employment, no schooling could have prepared me for the realities of being a merchant.

"Yes, you are right, I do follow my heart, and that will never change," I said. "I have worked hard and given it my very best. I have learned a lot. I also have a lot to learn, but I am proud of what I have accomplished in such a short period of time."

At that moment, when I spoke my truth out loud, explained my side, and trusted I would be all right no matter what Michael's reaction would be, I had made the journey from *fired to inspired*. Finally, all the struggles and lessons I learned paid off. I was able to stand up and speak my truth without fear.

Since Michael had not shared in the business or financial decisions at Funky Trunk and was not aware exactly what I was struggling with day to day, I let him know that, true or not, it was not OK to say I am not a good businessperson. Darn, it felt so good to stand up for myself! I am so blessed to have a husband who not only loves me unconditionally, but also loves me in spite of myself. I was starting to love me too.

It has been almost a year since we moved in with Crazy Carol. I know this merging of our three lives has not been easy for her, yet she makes room for us. Mom shared with me her fear of us taking over and her losing her ability to make her own decisions.

For us, the move has taken away our ability to make decisions on our own and finds us instead asking for permission. Mom has not been able to convert Michael to almond milk; however, she has successfully flipped him from Cheerios to oatmeal. We celebrate the small successes.

This entire process has been an opportunity for healing in our family. For that, I am grateful. It really does take a village, and we are building ours. My mom has been able to nurture me (and Michael) and jokes that she is a stay-at-home mom. She knows we are always here for her and she is not alone.

Nothing about living with Crazy Carol bothers Michael. He lives with two women who just want to make him happy. What a lucky Brit. The best thing to come out of this merger is that all three of us have become more health-conscious and are able to support each other to get healthy and strong. Good grief, at this rate, we might live forever (more on that later).

Fan the Flame

READY OR NOT: IT'S TIME TO STAND UP FOR YOURSELF! WHAT DECLARATION DO YOU NEED TO MAKE? WHAT DO YOU WANT/NEED TO TELL THE WORLD?

IS THERE A GAP BETWEEN HOW OTHERS MAY PERCEIVE YOU AND HOW YOU PERCEIVE YOURSELF?

MEET THE MANIFESTING MAVEN (THAT'S ME!)

From Fired to Inspired. My inspiration has come from God, the Universe, and my Shero (that's a female superhero, folks), Karen Drucker. Karen is a songwriter/musician from California. Her music has lifted my spirits for many, many years. Just ask the artists with whom I work; they'll tell you I play Karen's tunes at Funky Trunk constantly.

I don't know if I was on crack or what (I wasn't on crack, just Coca-Cola), but I got so excited when the opportunity came along for me to possibly meet Karen. I follow her email newsletters, and one day I got wind of a women's retreat she was planning in Hawaii. I said to myself, and everyone I knew, "I'm in!" It was time for some serious manifestation. They don't call me the manifesting maven for nothing.

Doubts crept in. The trip cost a lot of money, and besides the money, who was going to watch the shop for a week while I'm out meeting my musical idol on the islands? I had not been away from Funky Trunk Treasures that long since it opened. But, one day at a time, I started stashing money here and there. Funky Trunk artists pitched in by hosting a little fundraiser. Customers too tossed some bills in a tip jar on my counter marked, "*Wowie, Kim's going to Maui.*"

I made plans to travel with my friend Cheryl. Cheryl handled all the accommodations and reserved the rental car, which gave me more time to manifest some moola. Everything came together as it needed to, and my shop was left in good hands. Yet again … the Universe provided when I fearlessly moved forward. Cheryl planned it so well, we had a few days to relax and rest before the retreat at the Lumeria Resort in Maui began.

I was a little restless leaving my baby (the shop) behind. I figured Michael sure could use the break from me too, since I was so stressed out. Eventually, I was able to chill out and have some fun. Chilling out has never come naturally to me. Michael once said, "You couldn't relax if you were unconscious." I guess how to chill is a lesson I may never learn.

What a beautiful and amazing place the Lumeria Resort was for a retreat. The energy there was intoxicating. To save money, I had registered to share a room with someone while Cheryl had opted for a private room. I fantasized for months about the person I would share this experience with. Who was I destined to meet? What was she like? Where was she from? Would I snore louder than her? Would I drive her crazy? I was so excited about the adventure that awaited me.

When we arrived at the resort, my jaw dropped at its stunning beauty. The grounds were peaceful and inviting. I kept thinking, "*I'm staying here, in this beautiful place, and I'm going to meet my Shero. Wow, what did I do to deserve this?*" Followed by, "*Cancel that. I am here and am going to suck up every little morsel of this experience! No negative thoughts for me.*"

Cheryl and I went to register and were told our rooms weren't quite ready. We could make ourselves comfortable in the lobby or walk the grounds. I asked if my roommate had shown up yet, and that's when the Universe planted a big one on me.

"Oh, no, Ms. Cline, you will have your own room. We had some plumbing issues and had to do some rearranging." I stood there frozen thinking, "*Whhhaaaaatttt!?*" Did I hear the hostess correctly? I questioned her, asking in disbelief, "I'm getting my own room?" "Yes, you are. We hope you don't mind the wait," she replied. Wow, did I owe the Universe a big one on that. A trip to a fabulous place, get to be there with a good friend, get to see my music muse, and now a room of my own. It was almost too much for my brain to manage. And off I went to my own room.

By now, I think Cheryl may have been turning a little green with envy. She had paid full price for a private room. Sorry, Cheryl. I went on my merry way to find my room. On the way, I stretched out on the outside lounge. I may have looked like I was relaxed on the outside, but I was screaming with joy on the inside and trying to take small deep breaths to calm myself on the inside. This retreat was all about radical self-care, and it had just gotten off to a really great start.

I had started Weight Watchers a few weeks earlier, so I was grateful that we had fresh, healthful meals provided to us. On top of everything else, we had plenty of time between programs to enjoy quiet time or explore the island. I was overwhelmed with the choices of what there was to do here … I wanted to do it all! Now! But instead, I focused on honoring what my body and heart needed. All I had to do was listen to them.

Let me tell you, there is nothing like starting your day in a circle of 20 women in meditation, prayer, reflection, and song, led by Karen Drucker. I was introduced to her music when I worked with the Rev. Chris Jackson at Unity of the Palm Beaches more than 10 years prior. He and I

"I focused on honoring what my body and heart needed. All I had to do was listen."

were switching offices, cleaning and organizing, and I got first dibs on the CDs in there. I had heard how awesome Karen Drucker was, so I snagged every one of her CDs I could find.

Since then, I have enjoyed her music. For years I have diligently added to my collection. Each song is like a singing affirmation. Her music and lyrics simply resonate with my soul. It's usually the only music I play when I am in the shop because it makes me and everyone else who hears it happy.

One night during the retreat, Karen invited us participants to perform at Spirit Expressing. We could sing, read a poem, whatever we felt like sharing. I wanted to sing her song "Shine." Little did she know, I had all but adopted it as my personal anthem. I hesitated to perform it, and thought to myself, *"Singing one of Karen's songs at her retreat would be like cooking Italian food for an Italian … it's just not right."*

The night before the performance, I was seated close to the podium where Karen stood. She asked the group if anyone planned on singing "Shine" the next night. There was no response. So, she said, "OK, I will," and she turned up the music. Then, as if she could see my inner thoughts, she turned to me and said, "You do it," and tossed me the microphone. Everything happened so fast from there, I didn't have time to react. I just grabbed the mic and, let me tell you, I shined! When I finished the song, I was smiling and laughing. Karen, my musical Shero, really got me good. The reaction from the group was priceless.

You see, I had done such a great job of being calm and relaxed, they thought I was an introvert. Then when I burst out in song, they were initially shocked. As I continued to sing, they smiled. Then they cheered. It was one of the most fulfilling, creative moments of my life.

Let It Shine

I'm gonna be the first on the dance floor, the first to raise my hand.

The first to state my opinion, the first to take a stand.

I won't play it safe and wait for a sign,

I'm gonna throw myself out there and let my light shine.

Let it shine, let it shine, I let my big bright brilliant beam of radiant light shine.

I'll be on 'Oprah' and 'Conan', '60 Minutes' and 'The View'.

They'll all be talking about me and all the things I do.

I'll be the one who sets the bar, the one who's in the know.

'Vogue' will come to me to see where fashion trends will go.

'Cause I shine, yes I shine, I let my big bright brilliant beam of radiant light shine.

For too many years I hid my light, fearing I was too much

and who I was just wasn't right.

Then I heard this voice from within and up above saying

"You're here to be a shining light and give and receive love".

So now I'm going for my dreams, nothin's in my way.

"Carpe Diem" is my mantra, I practice kindness every day.

I take time to connect, take time to have fun,

I wanna know I've used up every drop before my life is done.

So I shine, yes I shine, I let my big bright brilliant beam of radiant light shine.

I am a woman of power, a woman of grace.

The life that I've lived is in every wrinkle on my face.

I love myself so I can love you too,

I know when we're connected there ain't nothin' we can't do.

So let's shine, let's all shine, Let's let our big bright brilliant beam of radiant light shine!

Fan the Flame

FAN THE FLAME:
LOGICALLY THERE WAS NO REASON THE HAWAII TRIP SHOULD HAVE WORKED OUT FOR ME, BUT IT DID.

HAVE YOU EVER SET YOUR SIGHTS ON A SEEMINGLY UNREACHABLE GOAL? HOW'D IT WORK OUT?

MY HUSBAND HAS SAID TO ME, "YOU COULDN'T RELAX IF YOU WERE UNCONSCIOUS." ARE YOU A HIGH-ENERGY GAL LIKE ME? HOW DO YOU RELAX?

WHAT CAN YOU DO TO BE MORE TRUSTING OF THE PATH YOU'RE ON?

WHAT SIGNS DO YOU THINK YOU NEED TO KNOW YOU'RE HEADED IN THE RIGHT DIRECTION?

FROM COMBUSTION TO REFLECTION: MORE CHANGES COME FOR FUNKY TRUNK

I am grateful to still have a connection to the women I shared the retreat with and for that magical experience the Universe provided in Hawaii. While there, I was able to slow down enough to know that I needed to make more life changes. It was time to take care of me.

In Hawaii, I did the math and realized I was working at Funky Trunk Treasures at least 75 hours each week. After-hours classes we had there and other events upped the number of hours I spent at my shop even further. I was approaching Funky Trunk's second anniversary, and I had yet to draw any income for myself. My days off were few and far between.

I did a lot of praying during that time in Hawaii. I prayed for guidance and support. By the way, when asking for guidance, I like to remind God that I don't always get the sign or message. He has to make the memo really obvious for me. I ask Him to please make it obvious or repeat, if necessary. I had a serious talk with God: *"If releasing Funky Trunk was in my highest good, I was willing to let it go. If I was to continue on this path, then I was willing to do the work, be a better businessperson, and create a life for myself outside of the shop."*

"I also realized that I was successful, had control, and had nothing to prove anymore."

I knew a lot of changes needed to be made personally and professionally when I got back. It was just something I had to do, no matter which path I chose. It was to let go what was no longer working or serving me well and begin to create the life I really wanted. I was empowering myself to act on my reflection.

Before leaving for the retreat, my friends and artists cautioned me that I was working way too many hours. Every time I heard that, I snickered, "No way! I am having way too much fun!" I was doing what I loved, using all my gifts to the fullest, engaging with customers and artists, organizing, marketing, merchandising, all mixed with the joy of supporting others. Life at Funky Trunk was a new adventure every day.

Once I became aware of how out-of-balance my life had become, I couldn't live that way anymore.

Let me introduce you to Baby Kim. Baby Kim can get a little cranky when she lacks rest and time to play with friends or family. I was cranky, but didn't have to be. I also realized that I was successful now, I had control of myself, and I had nothing to prove.

When I got back home from Maui, I was so excited and ready to put my realizations to work. I told my friend and bookkeeper Rhonda what I had discovered and how it changed my outlook. I told her, "By golly, I am taking time off for me … not one day, but two days a week … and I am going to pay myself too … and I am going to pay myself first." I paused ever so slightly between each declaration for her reaction or approval.

She was pleased at my newfound resilience. In her cute Kentucky drawl, she replied, "You know, Kim, you are getting ready to head into your busiest season." Man, she sure knew how to be a party pooper! *"Oh, yeah, that's right … duh,"* I thought.

"Then I will take time off after the first of the year, but I am paying myself now," I said. We both laughed.

Once I got back in town and settled a bit, I hit the ground running. I had done some internal clearing of my mind and consciousness, and now it was time to clear my environment. First thing? I had to release some artists from the shop. It was time for them to go, especially if their items were not selling. I knew neither of us was being served. But many of them didn't have the courage or ability to choose for themselves. It was difficult, but I did it.

Next, I re-merchandised the shop to change the energy in the space, and a customer and friend did a smudging (traditional cleansing technique from the Native Americans) to clear any negative energy left behind. I was open and willing to try anything that helped give my shop a fresh new start.

Fan the Flame

HOW CAN YOU RECALIBRATE AND TAKE TIME TO REFLECT?

CLOSE YOUR EYES, AND IMAGINE AN ALTERNATE REALITY FOR YOURSELF: ONE THAT LEAVES YOU FEELING ENERGIZED AND EXCITED.

WHAT'S THE FIRST STEP TO GETTING THERE?

AS YOU ANSWER EACH OF THE QUESTIONS IN THESE SECTIONS, YOU ARE INCREMENTALLY ENGAGING IN SOME INTERNAL CLEARING. CAN YOU FEEL IT?

NOW, WHAT IN YOUR ENVIRONMENT NEEDS TO CHANGE IN ORDER FOR YOU TO CONTINUE MOVING FORWARD?

THE PURPOSE OF THE FLAMES

What I realized after all the reflecting and cleansing is that I deserved to be compensated for my hard work. So, I began to pay myself. It sure felt empowering. I had gone from jobs where other people decided how much to pay me to being the business owner and deciding for myself what I deserved. I was free of my self-doubt.

And then, I augmented my team. Colleen is the director of first impressions and works on my days off, Sarah works events, and our FunkMaster Sheri coordinates musicians for what we call our "Funk Fest." With time, I have gotten pretty darn good at taking time off for me, and I love having a bit of money in my pocket for my efforts.

When I think of all that time I kept resisting saying, "I can't," and "No way," and letting fear paralyze me, I realize that it was such a waste of my time. I am happy to be moving forward. I find more peace and joy when I just let go.

I always thought I was a go-with-the-flow kind of gal, and I guess in many ways I still am. But now, when the stakes get higher, it seems like my resistance does as well. Over the past few years, I can hear myself saying,

"No way, I can't do this or I can't do that, or I can't move my shop." What I have found is that usually the things I resist doing eventually happen. Once I have the courage or guts to step up, trust, and go with the flow, it is always — without a doubt — for my highest good. I just couldn't see it at the time.

From experienced eyes, opening Funky Trunk Treasures was the easiest and fastest thing I have ever done. It's been rewarding in more ways than I can say. And now, I'm writing this book. I feel the same about this process, but with much more joy than I had when opening my shop. With this book, I have some idea and plan of how to get from point A to point B. I was quite clueless when I began Funky Trunk, at least on a conscious level. Why is it that in our lives, somewhere between birth and adulthood, we invite in the notion that everything has to be hard? Here's the truth: That's just a big fat lie.

Looking back at most of my adult life, there seemed to be a lack of money, time, support, and resources. Whatever came my way, I became a master at making lemonade out of lemons. Sounds good, right? So what if that went wrong? I could just ignore it and do this instead. Making lemonade is a great survival and coping mechanism, but it does tend to keep us stuck and unaware that we have the ability to change. We have the power to change. I had the power to change.

When I began to shift my thinking to empowering myself, I was unaware that somehow I began to create a most charmed life. Now I am doing what makes me happy. My life is filled with supportive and loving friends, I'm married to my Prince Charming, and I enjoy peaceful relationships with my mother and children. All of this is truly divine. Life is good and, strangely enough, the good life seems to have just sneaked up on me.

I have been married many times … five times. On one hand, people may say, *"Gee, Kim, you're not very good at being married."* But I *choose* to look at it differently now. With each of these men, with each of the experiences they shared with me, with each moment, I learned more about myself. I gained a lot of life experience and became what I was destined to become at this very moment in time.

As many years as I spent being married, I also spent many years as a single parent. This is where I learned to make the best of what I had, and to deal with it. I will say this, if I never see another ramen noodle in this lifetime, it will be too soon. I am so glad those days are behind me.

Years ago, my three girls and I were living in a subsidized apartment in South Florida. I used to play this game with them called Beat the Budget. Every time a bill came in the mail, we would look to see what the balance was and discuss if the bill was a fixed or flexible expense. If flexible, what could we do to lower that bill? For instance, on the electric bill, we could be mindful about turning off lights, put a timer on the hot-water heater, etc. What a brilliant mother I thought I was, getting the girls to help me save money. I didn't realize, at the time, the teaching moments I was creating.

My girls caught on. One day, I walked in after work to find my daughter Amanda standing on the kitchen table unscrewing light bulbs from the chandelier. I didn't want to startle her. As I walked toward her quickly and cautiously, I asked, "What are you doing?" She replied, "There are eight light bulbs in here, and we only need one."

I really didn't know whether to laugh or cry at that point, but I did feel proud. She got it. She got me. And she joined in the family's money-saving efforts. What a joy it is to see this magnified in my life today. People get me now, but I had to get me first.

> *"People get me now, but I had to get me first."*

Fan the Flame

IS IT TIME FOR YOU TO "JUST LET GO"?

WHAT'S FIRST ON YOUR LIST?

WHAT KEEPS YOU FROM LETTING GO?

WHAT BETTER REALITY IS AWAITING YOU ON THE OTHER SIDE OF THAT DECISION?

WHEN IS FEAR YOUR FRIEND, AND WHEN IS IT SIMPLY A ROADBLOCK TO YOUR MOST DIVINE LIFE?

CONFUSED NO MORE: REMOVING THE SMOKE SCREENS

What does a life-altering shift look like? When I used to think about it, I fantasized that the world would stop for a few moments, and an angel would simply descend from the sky to tell me what to do, and then gently point me in the right direction. There would be trumpets blaring and a bright, beautiful, white light illuminating my path.

But for me, and for most of us, that's not how it actually happens. The real shift happens slowly, piecemeal, and sometimes disguised as, "OMG, this sucks!" I've experienced many life-changing events that have happened over time, providing me opportunities to grow and shift. If and when I ignored the signs, the stakes got a little higher each time.

For me, I would describe the feeling as hitting the wall or, sometimes, rock bottom. Rock bottom is always a place of depression and despair. I've been there more times than I choose to remember, pulling myself up and doing my best to pick up the pieces.

> "Getting fired from my job took me to a breaking point where everything was stripped away and I was no longer able to fight or struggle."

I think the only reason I didn't try to check out of this world a long time ago was because I didn't want to leave my children behind with the feeling they didn't matter enough for me to live, or that I didn't love them enough to stay. Thank goodness for my strong sense of responsibility to my children. I am still here because of them, and my reward has been to see them blossom into the wonderful young women they are today.

There were times when I just couldn't smile and pretend everything was OK. In that black hole, I had no idea who I was, what I was, or what I could do to fix things. I am hardheaded, and have hit the wall a few times over the years. Some may argue that has made my head harder. Being solution-focused by nature, and a recovering co-dependent by nurture, I am good at fixing things and trying to make things "all better." I just didn't know how to fix me.

Getting fired from my job took me to a breaking point where everything was stripped away and I was no longer was able to fight or struggle against myself. But from that broken place, that dark hole, I reacted differently for the first time. I took a deep breath; I made a change; I allowed myself to become who I was meant to be and not what someone else saw or needed, or desired, or expected. I let go.

I didn't know what I was creating when I opened Funky Trunk Treasures, and almost every day I am made aware that the shop is not only a place that supports local artists, but a place where people are lifted up, inspired and comforted. For many who enter its doors, it's like coming home. Here, they have found a place to belong. And so have I.

Have you ever noticed how sometimes things just come together? That's *flow*. When I am in the flow, everything just falls into place. That's now the confirmation I look for. If things are flowing and falling into place, I know I am on the right path and I am co-creating with God. I spent too many years working hard to find solutions that weren't there and trying to fix things to the way I thought they should be. Now I know I was just spinning my wheels. We cannot out-think or out-give God. The good God creates is limitless.

Fan the Flame

WHEN HAVE YOU EXPERIENCED SIGNIFICANT "SHIFT" IN YOUR LIFE?

WHAT PART OF THAT SHIFT CHANGED YOU PERMANENTLY, FOR THE BETTER?

DO YOU BELIEVE ALL THINGS THAT HAPPEN IN YOUR LIFE ARE FOR A HIGHER PURPOSE? WHY OR WHY NOT?

WHEN YOU'RE IN YOUR "FLOW," HOW DO YOU KNOW? WHAT DOES IT FEEL LIKE?

HOW CAN YOU CREATE MORE FLOW IN

HONORING THE TEMPLE: IT'S TIME TO GET FIT

Last year, my friends, Vickie and Audra offered me a girl's weekend. They wanted me to join them for a half-marathon in Sarasota. They knew I wasn't taking much time off, and felt it would do me some good to get away for some fun. I could be a raging fan and cheer them on, or I could sleep in and get some much-needed rest. I said, yes. "Sounds like fun; I am in!" I squealed.

By the time that weekend rolled around, I had started taking two days off each week. I felt guilty about leaving someone to work the shop without me on a Saturday. I went anyway, because these young women are amazing. I knew it would be time well spent. Time for me. I was also consciously trying to work harder on relationships that mattered. It was important that I honor my commitment to join them for the weekend away, even if I felt it was a bit self-serving or selfish.

Vickie was behind the wheel, we were on the road, and Audra proceeded to give us the final version of the informational brochure (complete with clip art) she had created. It was an itinerary of our weekend.

(Her brochures are just one of the reasons why I love her.) As most women do, we chatted the entire way, ate, shopped, got a good night's rest, and yes, I slept in.

I thought about how sweet my friends were to invite me along for their race weekend. I was in awe of their commitment to running, and how they accepted me unconditionally. What a gift. That entire time, they were having fun, and that is something that always appealed to me. "Let me introduce you to Kim Possible. She's the one who attacks life with zest and enthusiasm, and she's always been inside me," I thought. Hanging out with these two runner girls reminded me that Kim Possible needed to get her groove back!

On the way back home, still lots to talk about (surprise), I said, "OK, girls, what would I have to do to go from point zero and be able to walk in a 5K?" Just nine months ago, I had walked to the stop sign at the end of the street. It was only four houses beyond our driveway, and I had to turn back. A 5K? What was I thinking?

I was stunned at my own question. I truly couldn't believe I had just asked it. But then, like they knew what was coming, cellphones were whipped out and the Internet searches began. Vickie found a workout plan, and I immediately scheduled each workout interval on my calendar. Then, we found a 5K that would be in our area on a date that would give me time to prepare. I registered right then and there on my phone! (Which, by the way, was a feat within itself.) Watch me go!

Here's the kicker: I never doubted for a second that I could do this. I knew I could because my friends told me I could, because I told me I could. No one said I couldn't, not even my inner voice that I've become tuned in to. So success was all I knew. I knew I had some physical challenges to overcome, but I knew that diet and exercise were the cure.

> "I knew I could because they told me I could. No one said I couldn't, so success was all I knew."

There was no way physical barriers would stop me. I was ready to break free.

I see clearly now how others' doubts about us can undermine our efforts and dreams. That is why we must learn to be selective with what we share and with whom we share it. I'm not saying someone would undermine us on purpose, not really, but everyone has his or her own stuff they're dealing with and they may not know the best way to "show up" for us and give what we need. Stop and think about how destructive your own negative talk is, and you should love yourself more than anyone! Love yourself; that will get you from the start to the finish line on any 5K.

Just 11 weeks ago as I am writing this book, I started a walking plan. I began outdoors and quickly went to the indoor treadmill. It's funny, all this time I thought the equipment sitting in front of the door was a burglar alarm. Who knew I could take a walk on it? Every week, my walking time increased.

Then, one day each week, there was a longer walk that I did outside with a friend. I also incorporated yoga and Zumba® into the mix whenever my schedule or body allowed. Let me clarify here: I'm not anywhere close to the proper positions or moves in these things, but I am getting there. I simply show up and do my best each time. Happy to say, I am thrilled to see the changes taking place both within me and in my physical appearance.

With all these fitness revelations, my energy levels are at a new high. In the past, I resented a doctor for looking at me and only seeing an obese person. He didn't take the time to look at my history or ask any questions. He just recommended that I eat just three meals a day. He is no longer my doctor; I deserve better than that and have moved on. I have sought out health professionals who support my health and wellness goals.

I remember several years ago, I ran into an acquaintance. She introduced me to her friend. All her friend saw in me was a fat person and a potential customer as she jumped right in to her testimony and sales pitch. She started telling me how she just lost a bunch of weight and how she could help me do the same. *"News flash, I just met you and didn't ask for help,"* I thought.

Personally, I believe anyone can lose weight on any plan when they are ready to do so. But changing our behaviors and keeping it off? Well, that is where the real work begins. I mean, who eats only because they're hungry? We relax around food, reward ourselves with food, comfort and celebrate with food. Shall I go on?

I have been a *P.H.A.T.* (pretty hot and tempting — lol) woman for years, resembling a Renaissance woman more than a magazine model. Being a voluptuous woman in Renaissance times was a sign of prosperity; that's why there are so many curvaceous women in the paintings from that era. I love me, and I have embraced my curves. If this is the package I've got, I will present it as best I can. My dream is not to be skinny or someone else's ideal body weight; my goal is to be healthy inside and out, so that I may enjoy all the abundance I have in my life. Weight loss is a beautiful side effect of the healthy choices I have incorporated into my life. It's not what I focus on.

The 5K I registered for was a big success. I enjoyed it so much, I registered for another one, and another. My friend and adamant Funky Trunk supporter Elizabeth invited me to join her on a trail run, too. Elizabeth had just had her third baby only months before, so I really thought I was going to be the one cheering her on, but *nooooo* (say it like Steve Martin, everybody), there she was leisurely walking ahead of me, enjoying the scenery, taking pictures, and encouraging me every step of the way. Whew, what a woman!

It just goes to show you, sometimes you're the windshield and sometimes you're the bug that hits it. I wasn't sure I was going to make it through this trail run. When a golf cart came up behind us, "You ladies doing all right?" I thought about jumping on, but I didn't. I kept going. I kept sweating and moving through the pain despite the man on the cart staring at my voluptuous behind. Elizabeth and I came in last place, but we finished the race. I believe that makes us winners.

Each and every day, I am amazed at what I have accomplished. I am excited to wake up, dress the part of a successful exerciser, and get on that treadmill. Really, I am committed to my walks. I get disappointed if I don't get some type of activity in on the non-walk days. Who is this person? Is this me? I mean, really!

One of the dreams I have tried to keep buried for years is to travel, to speak, and to inspire others. Now, I step back in amazement at what is transpiring in my life. How can I have stamina for traveling and speaking if I don't improve my physical condition? I will get there.

Fan the Flame

DO YOU HONOR YOUR BODY BY KEEPING IT FIT AND HEALTHY? HOW COULD YOU DO BETTER?

CAN YOU SIMULTANEOUSLY ACCEPT YOURSELF AS YOU ARE AND STRIVE TO IMPROVE YOURSELF?

HOW DOES THIS SHOW UP IN YOUR LIFE?

HAS ANYONE EVER ASSUMED YOU COULD DO SOMETHING AND BE SUCCESSFUL BEFORE YOU EVEN THOUGHT THAT ABOUT YOURSELF?

HAVE YOU SET A GOAL TO BE YOUR FIRST AND LOUDEST SUPPORTER FROM NOW ON?

ON FIRE AND INSPIRED...FOREVER

Once I committed to writing this book, physical and emotional challenges came out of nowhere. Proof, my friends tell me, that I am doing what I need to do. I am on my path, and there is an opportunity here to heal and grow. Baby steps? Not for me. Not anymore. I am putting myself out there with this book, and the process of writing it has brought up all kinds of past and present issues. I welcome them.

    Today, I anticipate with an open heart what will come next for me, what will further inspire me and others. I am open and receptive to my highest good. You've probably heard the saying, "When you are ready for the lesson, the teacher will appear." Let me tell you, my teachers have been lining up.

    I'm grateful for each and every one of my school teachers who acknowledged and supported me and my creativity. In recent years, teachers have come into my life in the form of artists, merchants, and friends.

    I'm grateful for every boss who modeled what I wanted and what I didn't want in my life, and for the ones who saw my potential and supported me to grow and develop leadership skills.

"I am open and receptive to my highest good."

I'm grateful for Tracey, who helps keep me tuned in to my spirit and who reminds me to go with the flow, especially when life gets a little wonky.

I'm grateful for Vickie and Audra, these smart fun ladies who have pushed me forward. They were so gentle, I didn't even realize they were pushing me. And they have no problem keeping me accountable either.

I'm grateful for my husbands who did the best that they could do at the time and who, like me, were searching for a family, a home, and a partner to share their life with. I am especially grateful for Michael, my Prince Charming, who has taught me what unconditional love is by his actions and undying support.

I'm grateful for my three daughters, Katy, Amanda, and Samantha. I am continually inspired by them as I watch them blossom with determination and courage along their life paths. They make me want to be a better person.

I'm grateful for my mother. Besides a lifetime of her wit and humor, she taught me that the good ol' boys were brought up to work together in teams. Girls, on the other hand, were raised to compete against each other, so we have to work harder to support one another. It's because of her that I have learned to cherish my female friends more and more.

I'm grateful for Sacha. She's my crown jewel, my bestie. She is an artist, life coach, author and speaker who always loves and supports me. OMG, don't look now, Kim Possible, but the Universe is conspiring to support you!

WHAT'S NEXT FOR KIM POSSIBLE?

The feelings of being fired now feel like ancient history. Today, I have the freedom I never knew was available to me. I have created balance for the first time in my life and have learned to accept help and embrace the people who show up in my life to assist me. I am surrounded by creativity in my environment every day. Each time people come into Funky Trunk Treasures and express their feelings about my shop, I feel a sense of pride. I realize that I made this happen. I take a moment to pause, smile and say, "Thank you."

I am filled with gratitude for my journey of devastated to divine. I have truly given birth to my happiness. My wish for you is the same. Courageously fan your flames and surround yourself with others who believe in you and will do the same. We need each other.

"I am filled with gratitude for my journey of devastated to divine."

Printed by Libri Plureos GmbH in Hamburg, Germany